MEDIA MANUALS

Continuity in Film and Video

MEDIA MANUALS

Continuity in Film and Video

A handbook for directors, script supervisors & PAs

Second Edition

Avril Rowlands

Illustrated by Colin Cant

FOCAL PRESS

Focal Press
An imprint of Butterworth–Heinemann Ltd
Linacre House, Jordan Hill, Oxford OX2 8DP

 PART OF REED INTERNATIONAL BOOKS

OXFORD   LONDON   GUILDFORD   BOSTON
MUNICH   NEW DELHI   SINGAPORE   SYDNEY
TOKYO   TORONTO   WELLINGTON

First published as *Script Continuity and the Production Secretary in Film and TV* 1977
Second edition 1989
Reprinted 1991

British Library Cataloguing in Publication Data
Rowlands, Avril
Continuity in film and video: a handbook for
directors, script supervisors and PAs – (Media
manuals). – 2nd ed.
1. Continuity. Cinema films – Manuals   2. Continuity
Television programmes – Manuals
I. Title   II. Rowlands, Avril. Script continuity and
the production secretary in film and TV.   III. Series
791.43′0233
ISBN 0 240 51290 1

Library of Congress Cataloguing in Publication Data
Rowlands, Avril
Continuity in film and video: a handbook for directors, script
supervisors and PAs/Avril Rowlands: Illustrated by Colin Cant. –
2nd ed.
      p.   cm. – (Media manuals)
Rev. ed. of: Script continuity and the production secretary in
film and TV. 2nd ed. 1977
ISBN 0–240–51290–1
1. Motion pictures – Production and direction.   2. Video
recordings – Production and direction.   3. Continuity.   I. Rowlands,
Avril. Script continuity and the production secretary in film and
TV.   II. Title.   III. Series.
PN1995.9.P7R67   1989   89–15794
791.43′0233–dc20   CIP

Printed and bound in Great Britain by the University Press, Cambridge

Contents

Preface

Since I first wrote *Script Continuity and the Production Secretary* in 1976 the world of film and television has undergone, and is still undergoing, a technological revolution which has brought about a major reappraisal of established ways of working and has meant taking on board many new techniques and terminology.

The one-time separate and mutually exclusive worlds of feature-film making and television have been forced to move closer together and rely on one another for support in an increasingly competitive world market. In the United Kingdom the monopolies of the BBC and ITV are fast becoming a thing of the past with the advent of cable and satellite television channels.

In this fast-changing world it is important and, in many ways, quite comforting to remember that the role of continuity remains unchanged. The PA or Script Supervisor might be logging timecode rather than slate numbers, but the job of specialised observation, which is central to single-camera shooting, stays the same. The medium used for recording the material—whether it is film, videotape, old bootlaces or, eventually, digital memory blocks—is irrelevant. If a film-style technique of single-camera shooting is employed, then the need for continuity remains.

In fact, the need today is greater than ever, due to the increasing sophistication of video, especially in the area of post-production. This has led to a wider use of videotape in single-camera shooting which has spilled over into industry, the home and areas of everyday life undreamt of a decade ago (except by the clever Mr Sony and his rivals in the Land of the Rising Sun!).

This new edition of my book aims not just to give the old one a new title and a new gloss by bringing it up to date in terms of the new technology but also to incorporate all that I have learnt over the past few years, both by doing the job myself and by teaching it.

I would like to dedicate this edition to the hundreds of people I have taught and to the many thousands more who bought the original edition. I would also like to thank everyone who has written or said nice things about the first book. I hope you find this new edition equally useful.

Inkberrow,
Worcestershire

Introduction

There you stand, dressed in your oldest jeans and thickest sweater (unless you're unbelievably lucky and start in fine weather): a stopwatch resting imposingly upon your bosom—maybe a Polaroid camera also—and a clipboard clutched as a lifeline in front of you. Pencils, ready sharpened, are secreted somewhere about your person; virginal continuity notes and unmarked pages of script lie neatly gathered under the clip on top of your clipboard, and securely tethered (in case of high winds) with a large rubber band. You have left your typewriter perched on a couple of packing cases in the cowshed nearby. You may, being prepared for any eventualities, have a sheet of plastic covering the paperwork. In your capacious waterproof bag somewhere near your feet are spare copies of the script and the schedule, together with spare pens, pencils, adhesive tape, scissors—spares of everything, in fact, even down to the odd aspirin and safety pin.

Around you are the rest of the unit, all equally uncomfortable despite the 'getting it together' drinks at the director's expense the previous evening. Everyone is bursting with the effort of being alert and appearing as impressive, busy and efficient as the others. One of the electricians cracks the first joke; the clapperboy comes up to you—or you go up to him—and he pledges to keep you informed of changes of camera roll. You, in turn, promise to keep an eagle eye on the slate numbers, and if he chalks up the wrong number, not to hold him up to general ridicule—at least, not in the first week of shooting. He says, not trying to be original, 'How about starting with Slate 1?' and you duly laugh and agree.

The cameraman, alternately gazing with a worried frown at the sky and then staring at his exposure meter and shaking it with incredulity, stops to ask the director: 'What's the first set-up?' The director interrupts his agitated first assistant, who is engaged in an earnest explanation of the lack of coffee/rolls/sausages and rushes over to his cameraman (who must be humoured). The first assistant has a go at the second assistant about the lack of coffee/rolls/sausages and the second assistant sends the third assistant off on a search. You become unwittingly involved with the boom operator who, under the guise of telling you the sound roll number—which, believe it or not, is roll one—starts to get too familiar. This does nothing for your image on the first day of filming, so you leap off to the director and look concerned and interested while he explains his first shot to the camera crew.

Artistes have now been called for, and appear in a flurry of make-up assistants with large powder puffs and dressers with large safety pins. The director and first assistant are smothered in a round of complaints and embracings and the air is full of expressions in vogue with top artistes. The rest of the unit stand round looking rather bored, except for the electrician who is looking round for likely talent.

Rehearsals commence, and you write down everything from the colour of the grass to the markings on the third rock on the left of frame. As rehearsals continue you neatly rub out what you first wrote as moves are changed, and then you rub out the second lot of notes as things change again.

1

Finally, all is ready for a take. The first assistant calls for quiet, the director calls 'turn over', the sound recordist calls 'speed', the camera operator 'mark it', and the clapperboy, who's been itching to do his bit with the clapperboard for the last minute, claps it and jumps out of the way. You having already written the scene, the slate, the description of the shot, the set-up and the artistes, are poised, one hand on the stopwatch, the other holding a razor sharp pencil.

The director calls 'action' and you're away. He almost instantly calls 'cut' due to heavy artillery fire from the army practice range two miles off. (The army wouldn't play ball and stop their activities for the filming.) The director casts a pained glance at the first assistant (who couldn't persuade the army); the first assistant casts a pained glance at the second assistant who hurries up to the third assistant (who has just arrived hotfoot and panting with the coffee etc.). The clapperboy painstakingly rubs out '1' and writes '2' on his board, with a stick of chalk embedded in a small piece of foam, attached to the clapperboard by a long clean piece of string. By the end of the shooting, the string is so well worn it has snapped off and the 'hunt the chalk' game takes place hourly.

You write 'NG, noise' on your notes—the board is clapped, the army silenced, the gaffer electrician stops work in protest as the coffee/rolls/ sausages meant for the crew have been used to bribe the army into silence, and your first day doing the job of continuity has started.

But what, in fact, is the job and how does one do it?

Note
Although I wanted to avoid any sexual stereotypes in this book, as there is not a suitable pronoun referring equally to 'he' and 'she', I have referred to the person doing the job of continuity as 'she'. I hope I will be forgiven for that or for any other apparent stereotypes. They are not intended.

Dressed sensibly and warmly and hung about with the trappings of the trade—clipboard, Polaroid camera, stopwatch, large canvas filming bag, etc.—you stand with eyes alert and pencil poised.

Out of Sequence Shooting: 1

When a film or video is being made it is not shot in a consecutive manner according to the story. That is, there is no progression from Scene 1 on Day 1 to Scene 25 on Day 25 or whenever shooting stops. It is generally shot out of sequence.

Take, for example, the following story:

Story

Two guards are on the battlements of a castle. It is daytime. They see a dusty rider on the road, galloping towards them. One guard reaches for his gun. The rider suddenly reins in his horse and looks up at the castle. We see the rider's view of the castle.

Cut to a shot of a woman on board ship.

Back to the battlements where one guard is keeping watch on the rider and the other guard runs down some stairs to raise the alarm.

Cut again to the woman on the ship.

Cut to a room in the castle, full of drunken guards. They hear the alarm, leap up and rush from the room.

In order to plan when you are going to shoot each separate piece, this story would be broken down initially into scenes:

Scenes in story order

Scene	Subject	Int./Ext.	Time
1.	Castle battlements	Exterior	Day
2.	Dusty rider on road (seen from castle)	"	"
3.	Castle battlements	"	"
4.	Dusty rider (from castle)	"	"
5.	Rider's viewpoint of castle	"	"
6.	Woman on ship	"	"
7.	Castle battlements. One guard exits Camera follows him down stairs	"	"
8.	Battlements. Guard raises gun	"	"
9.	Woman on ship	"	"
10.	Mess room of castle	Interior	Day

Scenes in story order:
1. Castle battlements; 2. Dusty rider; 3. Battlements; 4. Rider; 5. Rider's POV of castle;
6. Woman on ship; 7. Battlements. Guard exits; 8. Guard raises gun; 9. Woman on
ship; 10. Mess room of castle.

Out of Sequence Shooting: 2

Shooting in story order
If the shooting were to take place in that order there would be a great deal of time-consuming trudging up and down flights of steps for the whole unit with all the equipment. It would also mean that all the artistes would be required for the whole of the time, which would be expensive, and that all the locations would have to be in the same area, which is unlikely. So the script is broken down into a shooting plan.

Shooting plan
The plan or schedule for shooting is worked out bearing a number of things in mind.

Number of days
You might only have a specific number of days or weeks in which to shoot the story. You must try to fit the schedule into the requisite time allotted.

Position of locations
It takes time and a fair amount of organisation to move a unit from place to place. Therefore it is better to shoot everything in location A before moving to location B, regardless of the order in the script.

Location availability
If a particular location is only available on certain dates, the rest of the locations will have to be arranged accordingly.

Actor's availability
As with locations, if a particular artiste is engaged, the schedule will have to fit in with their prior engagements depending on their importance to the production.

Shooting schedule

Day		Scene	Location	Interior/ exterior	Time	Characters
1		6	Ship	Ext.	Day	Woman
		9	Ship	Ext.	Day	Woman
2	a.m.		*Unit move to castle location*			
	p.m.					
		1	Battlements of castle	Ext.	Day	2 guards
		3	Battlements of castle	Ext.	Day	2 guards
3		8	Battlements	Ext.	Day	1 guard
		7	Battlements and steps	Ext.	Day	2 guards
		2	Road (seen from battlements)	Ext.	Day	Rider and Horse
		4	Road (seen from battlements)	Ext.	Day	Rider and Horse
4		5	Road—LS castle	Ext.	Day	-
		10	Mess room	Int.	Day	20 soldiers

Shooting order

A shooting order like this allows for the fact that the ship is at a different location from the castle. It uses the artists economically (the woman is only engaged for one day's shooting), and the crew are not required to trudge up the steps to the battlements more than once, which allows a much faster shooting time.

Even the angles are often shot out of order.

Shots in Scenes Out of Order

A film or video is not only shot out of sequence but the shots within each scene are generally not taken in order.

To save time
This happens for a number of reasons, all to do with wasting as little time, and consequently money, as possible.

Usually only one camera is used and it has to be moved when different angles are shot. It is far faster to take all the shots from one particular area, whether they are from the beginning, middle or end of the sequence. The camera does not have to be moved around too much between shots and the lighting needs minimum adjustment until a major re-light is required for a totally different angle. Also props do not have to be constantly moved here and there to keep them out of the way of the camera, the lights and the vast army of people hiding behind the camera.

Part of a set
This set has been lit and the camera set up to take shots from one angle. Much time will be saved by taking all the shots needed from this area at the same time, irrespective of where they occur in the scene, rather than moving the equipment and lights from one side of the set to the other for each shot.

9

‹ of Continuity

onsible for continuity provides a complete, written document
ɟ. It should be a very detailed and accurate yet very concise
cise, I mean that while a two-page essay on each shot in a
flowiɲg   ᵣy style may be aesthetically pleasing it will be virtually useless as
a working document, as no one will have the time to read it for the required
information.

Use of document: (A) to unit on location
As the material is shot out of sequence it is obviously necessary to have some
record, built up over the shooting period, of what was actually shot in order to
preserve continuity from one shot to another and from scene to scene,
irrespective of the shooting order.

This means that the closest attention must be paid to every shot. A
description of the shot, how it begins and ends, the relationship between the
characters' actions to the dialogue, the position of props—in fact, as much of
what the camera sees as possible—must be written down for immediate and
later reference.

You might be asked by the cameraman to note down certain technical
information, such as the lens, the stop, distance and special filters. This would
assist him to match shots or compose retakes, but it only applies when
shooting on film.

Use of document: (B) to the film or videotape editor
The document also contains certain technical information which is of interest
only to the editor. Editors do not want to know details of costume and props, as
such notes are of use only while shooting is still taking place. But they are
interested in the reference point for the shot—the slate number in film or the 'in'
point of timecode in video—the shot description, the agreed take and, most
especially, the reason why a take was considered NG.

Back to the original story
The role of continuity ensures that when the finished material is assembled and
finally shown it will flow in chronological order in a smooth way, and that
continuity is preserved in action, sound, costume and props within each scene
and from one scene to another.

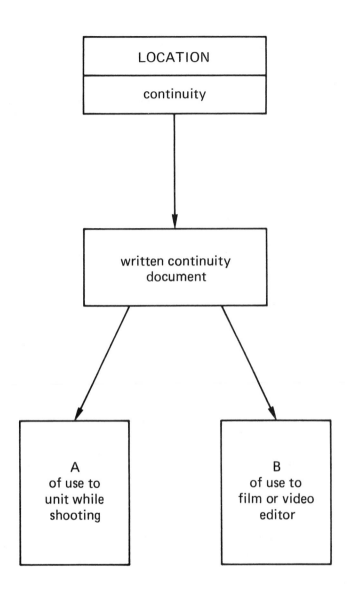

Continuity work
You provide a written record of the shooting. This document is built up while shooting takes place and is used as a reference. It is also of interest to the film or video editor for the technical information it contains.

Setting Up

There is a lot of work involved in setting up a production. Much of this might be undertaken by the person responsible for continuity on location, or it might be the responsibility of other staff. A lot depends upon the size and complexity of the production, past precedents and the type of company making the film or video.

In the feature-film industry, for example, the setting up is generally done by the **Production Co-ordinator**, while specific areas, such as location finding, casting and scheduling are undertaken by specialists in those fields. The **Script Supervisor** is solely responsible for continuity while on location.

In television much of the co-ordinating work in setting up a production is done by the **Production Assistant**, who is also responsible for continuity. (The additional multi-camera studio skills required by the PA working in television are covered in my other book, *The Production Assistant in TV and Video*.) Some aspects of the setting up might be the responsibility of a **Production Secretary**, whose work is largely office-based.

Independent production companies making programmes for television, commercials or pop promos will engage staff according to the size of the production. Smaller companies will most probably be content with one general dogsbody who does everything—and that job can be the most satisfying!

Industry will either use a facilities house for their productions or have their own 'in-house' video or film unit. A Production Secretary or Production Assistant is generally employed and their duties might well include continuity.

The setting up you are required to do might involve none, some or all of the following chapters, depending upon your own particular job.

Scripted or unscripted
The type of production which is to be shot will, of course, vary enormously, ranging from the multi-million-pound cinema epic to the video of the board meeting where the chairman gives his annual address. The requirement for continuity is there in both cases but to differing degrees. In this book I have divided productions into those that are scripted and those that are unscripted—drama and documentary types. The following chapters deal with the pre-shooting period of both types of production.

The life of the 'dogsbody' can be interesting and rewarding.

The Script

The first job in setting up—if you are working on a drama-type production—is to take a dog-eared, much-scribbled-over, almost indecipherable draft script and turn it into a nicely typed legible rehearsal script for everyone's use. This might not be the final, definitive version, but everyone wants something to work from as soon as possible.

Numbering

Every production is broken down into its smallest component—the script is divided into scenes and these, in turn, are separated into shots. It is therefore vital to number and label everything clearly.

Put the scene number and page number (i.e. Sc. II (13)) at the top and bottom right-hand side of each page. If there are a number of episodes you might find it useful to incorporate the episode number with the scene number (i.e. Episode 2, Scene 1 becomes 201; Episode 3, Scene 12 becomes 312, etc.).

Colour-coding

Colour-code different episodes by having each script photocopied on different colour paper.

Scenes

A change of location denotes a new scene. Always start a new scene on a fresh page, even if it is only one line.

Body of script

The script you type is a working document. You will be adding continuity notes to it during shooting and others will also require plenty of space for their own requirements. Type the script on the right-hand side of the page leaving a wide margin on the left; type stage directions in capital letters and dialogue in upper and lower case; and type dialogue in double space so that alterations can easily be made. Try not to carry over a piece of dialogue from one page to the next. The script should be typed single-sided only.

SCENE 506 : DAY. INT. OFFICE

LAURA IS SITTING BEHIND HER DESK, WHICH
IS LITTERED WITH PAPER AND PHOTOGRAPHS.
EVEN THE CHAIR IS FULL OF PAPERS. THERE
IS A KNOCK ON THE DOOR.

LAURA
Come in!

PAULINE ENTERS THE ROOM AND APPROACHES
LAURA'S DESK

PAULINE
I've come about the advertisement.

LAURA
Just a minute. (SHE FINISHES WHAT
SHE IS DOING THEN LOOKS UP)
Sorry about that. You've come about..?

PAULINE
The advertisement. You know, the one
in the paper.

LAURA
Oh, of course!

SHE SHAKES HANDS

Do sit down. Just put that junk anywhere.
I always work in an awful mess, don't
you? Now, you're...?

PAULINE
Pauline. Pauline Lunt.

Example of script layout.

Back to the desk.

Script Breakdown

After the script has been typed and distributed it is advisable to type a breakdown of the scenes. Such a breakdown will assist in working out the schedule of shooting and be useful to the set designer, costume and make-up supervisors, the property manager and many others. The breakdown should contain:

Page number and Scene number of the script.

Int/Ext: Day/Night

Is it an interior or exterior scene? Also, at what time of day is the action meant to be happening?

Location

Give the location; for instance, either 'garage' or the actual address if that is known.

Characters

List all the characters required in the scene, together with details of extras and walk-on parts.

Synopsis

It is helpful to give a brief synopsis of the scene. This enables people to work from the breakdown without having to constantly refer to the script. It is very useful.

Continuity

You might find it helpful to list whether there is direct or indirect continuity between scenes or characters. It will provide a guide to costume, make-up and props and be of use to you on location.

Props or notes

If you have room you could leave space for a prop list.

TITLE:

PAGE NO.	SCENE NO:	INT/EXT	DAY/NIGHT	LOCATION	CHARACTERS	SYNOPSIS	CONT.
1	1	Int	Day	Railway Station	Louis Alice Porter (W.On) Passengers	She meets him off train train. They arrange meeting in garden	No direct
3	2	Ext	Day	Gravel pit	Ch.Insp.Bartley James Wilcox Policemen	Police find body	No direct
4	3	Int	Night	Dining Room - Manners House	Alice / John James Wilcox Mary Wilcox Elwyn Brand Grant Tyler Sarah Glyn	Dinner party where Alice finds that Tew has been murdered. She is regarded with suspicion by James. Sarah & John exchange glances	Alice - direct cont. with Sc. 4 Everyone else - cont. with Sc. 5
10	4	Ext.	Night	Garden (by summerhouse)	Alice Louis	She tells him of her fears. He dismisses them as irrational.	Alice - back cont. with Sc. 3 - forward cont. with Sc. 5
13	5	Int.	Night	Dining Room - Manners House	John / James Mary / Elwyn Grant / Sarah Alice	Dinner party cont. Alice rejoins. James accuses her and Alice faints	Everyone with Sc. 3 Alice with Sc. 4

Script breakdown.

17

Timing the Script

Once the script has been finalised—for the time being at any rate—you should time it, noting down, scene by scene, the approximate durations.

You do this by reading it through to yourself, out loud, acting out the actions as they occur, i.e. 'goes to door'. Some scenes, of course, might prove rather difficult to act out, even in the privacy of your office or home. You will have to make an intelligent guess as to the length of those scenes.

Another guideline you can use is that 50 pages of script typed in the manner stated earlier and containing a mixture of dialogue and action will be approximately 30 minutes of final running time.

Time chart
Having timed the scenes, note them in chart form, adding up each scene to give a cumulative running time.

Read-through
The cast might be asked to attend a preliminary read-through of the script prior to shooting. This will be a good opportunity for you to get a more accurate timing.

Scene	Duration	Cumulative
1. Int. Living room	1.20	
2. Ext. Garden	2.00	3.00
3. Ext. Road	30	3.30
4. Int. Living room	4.20	7.50
5. Int. Hall	15	8.05
6. Ext. Car	40	8.45
7. Ext. Shopping City	1.10	9.55
8. Int. Shop (s'market)	3.05	13.00
9. Ext. S'ing City	45	13.45
10. Int. Shop (stationers)	25	14.10
11. Ext. Alleyway	30	14.40
12. Ext. Street	20	15.00

Example of time chart.

Artistes and How to Book Them

You need to book artistes quickly as the whole process takes some time to complete.

Artistes
Artistes come in all shapes and sizes and to suit all requirements. They are found by the producer and/or director, who either have definite ideas of what they want, or sit closeted for hours with directory and cast list laboriously trying to make a list of people to audition.

Agents
Artistes are looked after by agents, who find them work, look after their finances and generally administer to their needs. Some agents tend to specialise in actors with particular skills or abilities, others cater for all requirements. They can be pleasant and helpful or downright bloody-minded. They should be approached with caution.

Auditions
You might have to circulate the agencies, with details of the forthcoming production and a brief description of the cast needed. The agents then contact you with lists of people who they think suitable. After much discussion, you are given a shortlist of people to find out about. With this shortlist you ring the agencies and talk in deliberately vague and general terms in order to ascertain the availability of the person you are interested in for the dates necessary. Do not be specific because a verbal contract can be legally binding even if given over the telephone and without witnesses.

Auditions then take place with the selected people at a time and place previously arranged. After many such auditions, much discussion and countless references to the budget, a cast is agreed upon and contracts signed.*

Names and addresses
As soon as the principal artistes are booked, get their names, addresses and phone numbers without delay and circulate them to people like the costume and make-up designers, who will need to contact them.

Scripts and schedules
Let your artistes have scripts and schedules in good time—always supposing they are ready.

Hours of work
When you are actually shooting, keep a note of the hours the artistes work and their travel time to and from the locations, as they may be entitled to payment for working overtime.

*Pay attention to clauses in the contract relating to co-productions, repeat fees and special requirements (i.e. swimming required or hair not to be cut).

Artistes and their agents
Artistes come in all shapes ... and sizes. They are looked after by agents.

Extras and Walk-ons

The distinction between walk-ons and extras is often very fine but very important to the individuals concerned and has a bearing on the fees paid. A further complication is that the names differ between the BBC, commercial television and the feature-film industry.

The definitions given below are those used by the BBC. Commercial television has abolished the word 'extra' and uses 'Walk-on 1, 2 and 3' as appropriate, while the film industry only uses the word 'extra' but gives additional payments for extra responsibilities.

Definition of an extra
An extra is someone who, in conjunction with others, is given general directions, e.g.: 'mill about' or 'act angry', but no individual direction and has no set words. A crowd of fans at a football match might all be extras. They might applaud and cheer as the mood takes them, but they are not instructed beforehand on what to say and do not perform any specific pre-arranged actions on cue.

Definition of a Walk-on 1
Out of our football crowd one person might be singled out to wave a flag on cue. He will then be a Walk-on 1. So would the policeman who points a warning finger at the flag waver.

Definition of a Walk-on 2
If the policeman were given some unimportant, unscripted words to say, he would then become a Walk-On 2. So would the flag-waver, if he was told to utter some appropriate epithets at the policeman. If, of course, the words are scripted, then the Walk-On 2 becomes an Artiste and is paid accordingly.

Where to obtain extras and walk-ons
Extras and walk-ons are employed by agencies and can be ordered in bulk. You can ask for 50 peasants, assorted, 20 female, 30 male, between the ages of 25 and 50, or be more specific in your requirements.

There are agencies that specialise in certain types, for example, there is one which caters for stunt men, heavies and fall guys in general, and will produce a fine range of villainous-looking characters at a moment's notice.

Don't get carried away
It can be a fairly heady business, ordering vast quantities of people, and one must be careful not to get carried away by the experience, and over-order. You must also be careful not to make mistakes because although extras are not costly individually, *en masse* the price can be formidable, especially if overtime work is incurred.

Suitable transport must be arranged and clear instructions on rendezvous points given. It is usually necessary for them to be 'chaperoned' constantly, and usually someone is detailed to keep an eye on them and have them at the right place at the right time.

Always check and double check where extras are concerned. It is so easy to lose the odd one or two.

Film extras

1. An *EXTRA* is a human prop.

2. If an extra performs an action he becomes a *WALK ON 1*.

3. If, in addition, he says a few unscripted words he then becomes a WALK ON 2.

Children and Animals: 1

If at all possible, avoid children and animals. They are complicated to book, have an enormous number of rules and restrictions attached to their use and need a lot of looking after—even though they come with a retinue of chaperones, tutors, trainers and handlers. Often their minders can prove more of a problem to organise than they are.

Children and animals can waste an immense amount of time during shooting. On balance, I prefer children because at least (if they are old enough) they understand what you are saying—but trying to make an animal do something on cue requires superhuman effort and patience—and a flexible shooting schedule.

Where to find children
Children come from two sources, stage schools and non-stage schools. Much can be said for and against both.

Some directors never seek children at stage schools, preferring to make the rounds of ordinary schools and engage the help of drama organisers. Others cast solely from stage schools as they feel that the children will have a certain knowledge of the business and sense of discipline to start with.

Wherever they come from, in the UK if they are under 16 they need licences from the local education authorities before they can appear in films.

Licences
Before the licences are granted, the authorities have to ensure that the *Children (Performances) Regulations 1968* will not be contravened. An application form for a licence has to be filled in and submitted, and this form goes into searching detail about every aspect of the shooting.

Children and animals

Children and animals can both be difficult to work with. Both need more time than the usual shooting schedule can allow and vast amounts of patience.

25

Children and Animals: 2

Regulations

The regulations governing the use of children are very stringent, and should be examined in some detail before any individuals are booked and the shooting schedule arranged. Children's hours of work, tuition, rest periods etc. are all laid down quite categorically and must be adhered to.

When shooting, their hours must be carefully noted down as these details may be subject to inspection by the Education Authority.

Chaperones and tutors

Children under 16 need chaperones. These august ladies are to be found on any set sitting in a corner, knitting and discussing in depth how this production compares with the last, and exchanging the latest piece of gossip. They are in overall charge of the children. They must collect them from their home or their school, travel with them, keep an eye on them when shooting and make sure that they are not getting overtired or being worked for too long without a rest. They are very important to the children as they are not connected with the production and therefore acting solely in the child's interest. They must also take them home, or be responsible for them in the evenings if away from home.

If the shooting occurs during school term time, tutors must be engaged to give a specified number of hours schooling each day.

Animals

Animals can be obtained from a number of places. There are a few agencies which deal in them, otherwise zoos, circuses and nature reserves are all possible places to search for the animal required.

They almost always come accompanied by a trainer or handler. The problems with animals start with their first day's shooting. They do not present any of the problems with regulations one encounters with children.

The provider of performing animals in the UK has to comply with the *Performing Animals (Regulation) Act of 1925* in regard to training the animals.

Officers from the local authority have the right to inspect the premises with the object of preventing cruelty to animals.

1

2

Regulations for employing children and animals
There are numerous regulations governing the employment of children and animals.
They should be studied well. Any person under the age of 16 is classed as a child and
is subject to these regulations. All children must be provided with qualified
chaperones. All animals must be attended by their handler or trainer.

Locations: 1

You probably do not have much, if anything, to do with finding locations, but once they have been found, it falls on you to tie up the 'loose ends'—to get agreements in writing and arrange indemnity against heavy-handed crews damaging the surroundings in which they work.

How to find your location
It is interesting, however, to know how locations are found, and why you ended up for ten weeks at a rural one with an unpronounceable name which is not shown on any ordinary map.

What to look for
1. *The script.* The script is obviously the first pointer. If the story is set in one of the hotter, dustier regions of Spain, it is no good trying to shoot it just outside London. You might well find a dusty region there, but what about the weather?

2. *Accessibility.* It is possible to take a unit anywhere (almost). What must be considered is whether the cost and difficulties of travel to remote regions are worth while for guaranteed quiet, good weather and no one officiously demanding a permit.

A unit, complete with artistes, make-up, wardrobe, props, lighting, camera crew, etc., is a very large, cumbersome body to move around. There is usually some very heavy equipment, large vehicles and a large number of people.

3. *Communications.* This leads off from the last point. It is necessary to have fairly fast, reliable communications with civilisation, and there must either be a means of transport available or special transport provided often at great expense.

4. *Facilities.* You may get all the peace and quiet needed in Outer Mongolia, but what about the hotels, the lack of electricity, or even the availability of public conveniences? This is to say nothing of evening entertainment; although a good unit will always provide its own in one way or another.

Hunting for locations

Many things must be taken into consideration when looking for locations—not just peace and quiet. Reasonable accessibility to civilisation is one factor as a unit is usually quite a large cumbersome body to move around.

Locations: 2

5. *Weather.* This is a difficulty that haunts many location-hunters in this and some other countries. Sometimes, time wasted in waiting for the weather to settle could have been better spent in transporting everyone to a warmer climate. In most cases, it is not important to have particularly good weather. But it should be consistent in scenes that are to be intercut.

6. *Noise.* This can be another problem. These days you have to travel further and further away from population centres to obtain real silence, and then you face other problems. It is amazing how noisy the heart of the country is, what with birds, insects, tractors, animals and so on, even when you think it is quiet.

7. *Friendliness of the locals.* You may have found the ideal spot—it is reasonably quiet, the weather is very good, the scenery just right and there are hotels just up the road . . . but when you arrive, you are met by an assortment of hostile people, brandishing umbrellas, rolling pins or other weapons, demanding:

(a) that you leave immediately,
(b) that you agree to pay large sums of money as 'protection'.
(c) that the crowd are all given parts—speaking ones of course.

If you were finding locations, those are the sort of problems you might encounter.

Studios

Studios, by comparison, are a haven of rest. Everything is there to hand. But more and more productions—at least the exterior scenes—are being shot on location and the luxury of the studio sets is not to be taken for granted.

Locations: other aspects

1. Weather is an important factor. A run of bad weather can prolong a shooting schedule alarmingly.

1

2. Noise is another problem to be aware of if you are shooting sync sound.

2

3. Friendliness of the locals—it helps ease the strain.

3

Accommodation

Booking suitable accommodation is often a very complicated business. It is essential to take time and trouble over it and to check and recheck the situation constantly.

It is better to overbook, initially, rather than omit to make bookings for people, as no-one would take kindly to your muttered 'I'm sorry, I forgot', if they have no bed for the night. But do not forget to cancel the rooms not needed, otherwise there will be an unnecessarily heavy charge.

Finding what is available
Get as much information as you can about the available accommodation in the area where you will be shooting. Check whether you have to contend with the holiday season, the local carnival or the annual pole vaulting contest. If there is likely to be a shortage, make a block booking quickly and sort out the details later.

Finding the hotels
It is often not easy to find hotels close enough to the location that are satisfactory for price and number and size of rooms, and that can also meet all the varied requirements of such a varied group of people.

Making the booking
If it is a large booking, or made for a long period, many hotels come to some arrangement over a reduction in price.

Find out who wants what—for example, single rooms, single rooms with bathroom, double rooms etc. and try to arrange for these preferences to be upheld. It is not always possible, but if everyone is happy in their accommodation, it makes a lot of difference to the spirits and morale of the whole unit.

Some of the unit may well prefer to make their own arrangements. So long as this is acceptable to the director, they should not be forced to accept the booking you have made for them just because it simplifies things for you.

Your own booking
Make sure that you have adequate room in which to spread yourself and your mini office and, if you are likely to be knee-deep in mud all day, you might prefer your own bathroom as well.

Where to sleep everyone
Trying to find accommodation to suit everyone can be difficult. Apart from the practicalities of booking enough beds on the requisite nights in reasonable hotels you always get problems with some members of the unit who will never be satisfied with your arrangements.

Travel

It is very difficult to give specific details of what transport you will need and when. It depends so much on where your locations are, how many people prefer to make their own arrangements for travel and so on.

All you can really do is ensure that every single person on the unit has some means of travelling to the location—and that you have adequate transport actually on the location.

Travelling abroad

If shooting abroad, make sure all travel arrangements are made in good time, as air and shipping lines tend to get booked up quickly.

Do not forget to make arrangements for travel to and from the airport or port—coaches, buses, vans, cars, taxis etc. must all be booked.

Check up on everybody's passport, and arrange visas if necessary. If vaccinations or inoculations are needed, find out what is required and make arrangements for everyone. Adequate amounts—and a good bit over—of foreign currency will be needed.

Travel in this country

Make sure there is more than adequate transport. If 15 people are to be collected from Point A and taken to Point B, book something slightly larger than a 15 seater coach as there may always be one or two extra people who turn up at the last moment.

In arranging transport you often have to hire all kinds of vehicles, fix rail tickets, and most important, give clear rendezvous points and times for transport and people.

Find out the local taxi or car hire firm in the area where you are shooting and keep a note of their phone number.

Car parking

Make sure that there is enough car parking space available at the hotel and at the location—or find out where vehicles can be left, not too far from the location.

Transport
Arrange suitable transport for everyone whatever the location, or make sure they have equally suitable means of transport of their own.

35

Food (or to location cater or not . . .)

After accommodation and travel, food is one of the priorities. A number of firms specialise in feeding hungry units, from around 20 to unlimited numbers of people.

They operate from anything from converted buses, converted coaches and old lorries to the latest streamlined, fully equipped modern kitchen-on-wheels.

I cannot answer for all of them, but the ones I have experienced have all provided an excellent service—often rather too good in respect of one's waistline.

They are not cheap, but they do provide coffee and hot snacks in the morning, a full hot lunch, and tea and cakes and biscuits in the afternoon. And the time saved in having hot food ready to hand, rather than hunting around for pubs and cafes, is well worth it. The only thing lacking can be a suitable place for consuming the food, and the spectacle of members of a unit trying to shield their steaming plates from the elements—usually rain—while making a dash from the caterers' van to the nearest cover must have amused many a local inhabitant.

Other types of catering

If location catering is not to be provided, then find out in advance what restaurants and cafes are in the vicinity. See whether any of them could cater for the numbers and type of meal you require and make advance arrangements with them.

Do not forget that while *your* lunchtime meal may consist of a piece of crispbread and some cheese, many people on the unit demand something far more substantial, especially after a long, cold morning shooting in the open.

Other meal breaks

If your shooting schedule covers other meals, i.e. breakfast or dinner, make similar arrangements with a local restaurant. If you have no caterers with you, arrange to take flasks of coffee and tea for mid-morning and afternoon, and do not forget the paper cups, spoons and sugar.

If you are far from civilisation

There may be times when you find yourself shooting in remote areas with no food available from any source. There is only one answer and that is to carry your own packed lunch. This is not popular with units and if you are forced to provide sandwiches made the night before by your hotel, for consumption by a hungry crew, do at least take flasks of hot soup and coffee with you.

Location catering
Location caterers operate in a variety of vehicles and produce nourishing meals. They are usually very good value for the price.

The difficulty comes in trying to eat this tasty food while perched on the bonnet of a car doubled up to keep the rain from reducing your food to a sodden mess.

Costume and Make-up

While things are daily getting busier in the production office, others are working equally hard in their own fields.

Costume

The first thing the costume designer does is to read the scripts and make notes on the period and the type of costumes needed. If it is to be a period production, much research will follow to ensure historical accuracy down to the smallest detail.

Consultations follow with the director over the designer's ideas, and agreement reached.

The designer notes the continuity of dress from one scene to another in the script and a careful watch is kept on this during the shooting.

As soon as the artistes are booked, they are contacted, and measurements taken and discussions held with them. They often have to attend a number of fittings as the work of making costumes progresses.

Moving all the costumes around is a sizeable operation. Often location work can mean cramped, inadequate room for storage, washing, ironing and changing.

As with most things, speed is essential, and it is quite a feat to have a couple of coachloads of extras changed and on the set in double quick time.

Make-up

The make-up artist also reads through the script carefully to determine the period and type of make-up needed. Research is done and notes made on any special make-up, like beards, wigs etc. and any peculiarities relating to continuity, for example, a wound that gradually heals over a number of scenes.

The artistes are contacted in the same way as for costume.

During shooting the make-up assistants constantly hover round the set ready to touch up make-up that is wilting under the lights.

Costume and make-up
Costume have their own problems contending with unusual shaped garments and unusual shaped actors, while Make-up orders wigs, and researches into the correct make-up for the period.

Props and Design

Props that are to be used in the action, i.e. a chair that is lifted in a threatening way or a book that is picked up and read, are called 'action props'. These are organised by the appropriate person, who might be the second or third assistant director, or the assistant floor manager.

Other props that are not directly used in the action but are there merely as set decoration are called 'dressing props' and are the responsbility of the art director or designer, as part of the general design of the set.

Action props

The person dealing with them will have gone carefully through the script and the breakdown, marking all the props that are mentioned, i.e. 'JOHN PICKS UP THE BOTTLE OF INK AND THROWS IT ACROSS THE ROOM'. He works out the continuity of such props from one scene to another, i.e. in the scene following the ink throwing, there is no great time lapse, and there should be a large ink stain on the floor.

He also works out props that are not specifically mentioned in the script, i.e. 'MARY IS MAKING A LARGE APPLE PIE'. For that he needs to get all the utensils and ingredients to make the action possible. There must be sufficient supplies to cover any retakes.

He works closely with the art director as the props needed in the action must correspond in style and type to the general dressing of the set.

Design

Much research goes into the period and mood of a production, especially when shooting interiors, whether specially constructed at a studio, or adapted from existing buildings.

Exteriors are simpler unless they are specially constructed streets, house fronts and so on.

Design and props
This set shows the integral part design and props play in the director's overall concept of the production. A great deal of creative effort and research has gone into the design and construction of it.

Shooting Schedule: 1

The focal point of setting up for location shooting is the preparation and assistance in compiling the schedule. This schedule is the consummation of all the preparatory work.

It will comprise all the different pieces of information gathered over the weeks regarding every single aspect of the shooting as well as the day-to-day schedule.

It is a very important compilation, which is sent to everyone associated in any way with the shooting.

Front page
The front page should give the details of the production, the name, the job number, the dates, and also the names and phone numbers of all the unit and everyone connected with the production in a technical capacity.

Cast list
Give an accurate cast list, with the names of all the artistes and extras. You might also like to give their agents' telephone numbers on this page. Do not give the private phone numbers of the artistes, as the schedule will be widely distributed and the artistes might be undesirably harassed if the numbers were too generally known.

Travel
Give detailed information on the travel arrangements that have been made including the times and places transport departs for the location, and lists of the people to travel at that time.

If there is a train service, copy out a train timetable from the principal towns to the location.

For those using their own transport and for guidance to the crews it might prove useful to include maps with the schedule, or at least explicit instructions on how to get there.

Accommodation
Give a full accommodation list, with the hotels' addresses, telephone numbers and prices of the rooms.

Location and contacts
List all the locations, their addresses and people to contact in connection with them. Also some useful addresses and phone numbers would include the local hospital, doctor, hire car or taxi service and police station.

Production Number : 102/XYZ 1234

23rd March 1989 - 2nd May 1989

LOCATIONS: LONDON, READING, DIDCOT

SPIDERS IN THE BATH

by

John Graveney

DIRECTED by LORNA SHELTON

PRODUCER   .... JONATHAN WHITEHEAD
PRODUCTION SECRETARY .... PAMELA LOW
STORY EDITOR .... JANE GLOVER
PRODUCTION ASSOCIATE .... ANDREW MCGOUGH
FLOOR MANAGER .... JAMES DELTON
LOCATION MANAGER .... ELIZABETH DEAN
PRODUCTION ASSISTANT .... CHRISTINE TURNHAM
STAGE MANAGER .... BILL SMITH

DESIGNER .... LESLIE JOHNSON
COSTUME DESIGNER .... PETER HUNTLY-SMYTH
COSTUME ASSISTANT .... JOANNA WRIGHT
DRESSERS .... SALLY DOWNER/TED SMYTHE
MAKE-UP ARTIST .... SUZIE COX
MAKE-UP ASSISTANTS .... JANE LOWTON/MARY JENKINS

PRODUCTION BUYER .... TED BARCLAY

LIGHTING CAMERAMAN .... FREDERICK SELBY
CAMERA OPERATOR .... JACK WILLIAMS
CAMERA ASSISTANT .... KEITH SHINER
SOUND RECORDIST .... GRAHAM ASH
SOUND ASSISTANT .... HUGH BARBER
GRIPS .... GEOFF MORGAN
GAFFER SPARKS .... LES WOLFE

FILM EDITOR .... JUDY JOHNSON

The front page of a shooting schedule.

Shooting Schedule: 2

The way you set out the details of what scenes are to be shot each day is very much a matter of individual preference—yours and the production manager's.

A day to a page
It is sometimes thought simpler to type each day's details on a separate page, which can then be discarded when it is completed.

A week to a page
Others believe that the least amount of paperwork the better, and that it is far clearer to give all the information on as few pages as possible.

Whatever format you favour, there are certain things you must write down:

Rendezvous
Clear instructions on the rendezvous time and place. I have stressed in earlier sections how important this is, as most problems can be sorted out, provided everyone meets up at the beginning.

Shooting order
The shooting order will have been worked out on the basis of the speed of shooting, availability of artistes and locations, making the best possible use of the time available.

This shooting order commences with the date on which you are shooting, the scene or scenes you are shooting and then all the relevant details pertaining to those scenes, i.e.: the location, the characters involved in the scene, the time of day of the scene, and whether it is an interior or an exterior. You might also like to put details of the action props to be used.

Rescheduling
While the schedule should be as full a document as possible, changes may become necessary some time during the course of the shooting. You might be held up by the weather, or unforeseen circumstances may force you to make alterations. You might even reach the stage where a complete re-scheduling is unavoidable. If that happens, do check up that any necessary alterations to hotel bookings, transport etc. are made.

The really important thing about the setting-up period is that you should plan for possible contingencies, but if the 'impossible' happens, you should be flexible enough to be able to change things drastically if need be.

0830   MINI-BUS DEPARTS HOTEL, PORTHCAWL

0900   UNIT CALL ON LOCATION

1230   LUNCH

1800   approx.   WRAP

LOCATION   43 CHURCH ROAD, PONTYPRIDD, GLAMORGAN

CONTACT   Mr P. Jones (address above, no telephone)

EPISODE SCENE PAGE	LOCATION	CHARACTER	NOTES
412 (37)	Ext. Day. Hillside	Carrie Nick Auntie Lou Mr Evans	
305 (20)	Int. Night. Bedroom	Carrie Nick	
212 (33)	Int. Night. "	Carrie Nick	
209 (28)	Int. Night. "	Carrie Nick	

TECHNICAL REQUIREMENTS

Black drapes

2nd camera arriving in evening

WEEK 9
MONDAY 3 DECEMBER

Different styles of filming schedules.

You are not always in a drama situation.

Documentary-type Productions

The work in setting up an unscripted, documentary-type production follows much the same pattern as for something scripted. Locations have to be found, crews and artistes booked and travel, accommodation, catering, etc. arranged. There is, however, an additional aspect to setting up which might involve you to a greater or lesser degree.

Research
Research is the basis of preparation for much documentary filming and your taste for detective work will determine whether you enjoy being involved in documentaries.

The extent to which you are involved in the research depends on who you work for. If you are condemned to 'minding the phone' and typing the letters and given no scope in the preliminary research, you will understandably be bored and frustrated—unless you like phone-minding and letter typing as a full time occupation.

Learning about new things
The aspect I particularly like about the work is the amount you learn about subjects of which you were formerly ignorant. You might well have been ignorant of the subject as it never interested you. You might indeed view with extreme scepticism, as I did, the prospect of a few months research into the history of a famous football stadium, if, like me, you have always kept well clear of organised sport.

But by the end of the research period I was ready to admit that I had learned a good deal that was fascinating about the subject.

46

Documentary shooting
Research into documentaries can give you an insight into subjects you might never otherwise explore.

'Find Out All You Can About . . .'

You have started work on a documentary about '. . .'. You have been given the above directive. Where do you begin?

The subject
Obviously the subject of the documentary will give you the first lead.

Example 1: The history of aviation
A production about the history of aviation could take you on a lengthy journey through libraries, film and video libraries, museums, the air forces of various countries, the historic societies devoted to preserving old planes, etc.

Example 2: The sun-worshippers of S.E. London
A production about the sun-worshippers of South East London will take you to South East London (probably at dawn) to witness the worshippers in action—to a second floor flat in Camberwell which houses the headquarters of the sect—to the libraries for some historical background and to the local newspaper who first brought the subject to light.

Example 3: The training of nurses
A production on the training of nurses would take you to various teaching hospitals, to the library for some background to nursing manuals, and to much discussion with teachers and trainee nurses.

Once you know the subject, you can start researching into the most obvious aspects and other paths of exploration will open up.

The more you dig around, the more you uncover, and the amount of time, energy and patience you devote to the subject depends on the needs of the production and your instinct as a bloodhound.

Other bodies for research
Below is a short list of places which might prove helpful in beginning your research:

Libraries
Town halls
Local councils
Government departments
Law courts
Welfare institutions
Army/Navy/Air Forces
Universities
Polytechnics
Newspapers (national and local)
Film and video libraries

Research
Libraries can be useful starting points for research.

What to Take on Location . . .

As you look round your office with its well-stocked cupboards and shelves, it is very difficult to envisage exactly what you need to take with you on location, and the quantities required. Of course, very much depends on where you are going and for how long, but a selection of the following might be useful:

Scripts and schedules
Always take plenty of these as people are apt to leave them in the most extraordinary places.

Anything to do with the production
Any files specifically related to the production, e.g.: your production file, address book and diary must be taken.

Stationery and forms
If you use any standard forms, for example to do with artistes' hours etc., take enough of them, and a small amount of general stationery—notepaper, carbon paper, envelopes and stamps.

Miscellaneous
Here is a list of easily forgotten odds and ends which you would regret leaving behind.

Typewriter, Clipboard, Hole puncher, Stapler & staples, Adhesive tape, Paper and bulldog clips, Pencils/ball pens, Pencil sharpener, Eraser, Ruler, Rubber bands, Spare files, Spare folders, Rough paper, String, Scissors.

In addition for continuity
If your job is combined with that of continuity, take in addition:

Continuity report forms
1 set of coverage scripts
1 set of rough continuity scripts
1 set of scripts (to be interleaved with continuity notes for your daily use)
Progress report forms
Stopwatch
Polaroid camera and film
Daily continuity log forms
A plastic sheet to keep your notes dry in the rain
A small folding stool.

Packing up your office
Do not take too much away with you. You only have the problem of transporting it around from location to location and then probably taking most of it home unused at the end. Work out a list of essentials beforehand and stick to it.

. . . and Don't Forget the Boots . . .

Having packed your mini office to your satisfaction, what about your own belongings? Obviously, I cannot give any specific lists, but below are a few suggestions:

Warm or tropical countries
Suitable clothes, remembering that it is easy to give offence when shooting in countries where dress is related to religious or cultural practice.
Malaria tablets, or whatever preventative medication is advised.
Insect repellent.
A hat with a wide brim.
Sunglasses
Protective sun cream.

Cold countries (including the UK at most times of the year)
Warm clothes, thick sweaters, a windbreaker, thermals, a warm hat and scarf and . . . a pair of stout boots.

Don't forget that while most of the unit can go and warm themselves from time to time, if shooting is taking place, you are stuck there on the windy ridge or in the damp forest or wherever, and after a couple of hours you will be frozen.

If you have ever secretly harboured the idea that location work is in any way 'glamorous', you can forget it. It has all kinds of attractions but there can be nothing less appealing than, say, waddling out to a night shoot dressed in every available garment and hardly able to walk with the weight.

Dress for the job

When packing to go away filming, make sure you take suitable clothes for the conditions you are likely to encounter. Be prepared for hours of standing in the coldest and wettest places.

Specialised Observation

Having set up the production, you turn up on location on the first day of shooting and do ... what? What is the first requisite for doing the job of continuity?

Before writing the continuity report you must observe what is happening in each shot. So the paramount requirement for the job is having the ability to observe, to notice things. But it is wrong to say 'observation' and leave it at that. One is observing things all the time—certain things make an impression and are retained *in some form or another* in the brain, while other things are seen, but in a generalised way, and no clear imprint is made.

Accurate observation

No two people retain the identical impression of a scene or event. Eye-witnesses at a road accident, for example, are notorious for the diversity of their reports of the same collision. But you can train yourself, or be trained, to observe specific things accurately. Some women workers on egg inspecting lines do nothing but watch eggs pass in front of a strong light, and they are trained to spot defects. Policemen are trained to give fast, accurate descriptions of people. They note certain things; height, build, colouring, clean-shaven or bearded, shape of head, clothes and so on. Likewise with continuity; there are specific things to observe and after a while it becomes second nature to note them.

Much of what you see throughout the day makes only the haziest imprint on the brain. You go into an unfamiliar room. Your eye is caught by a painting on the wall and you remember it afterwards with great clarity, while only having the vaguest impression of the rest of the surroundings.

Training in observation

When looking at continuity in single-camera shooting you train yourself to notice not the random picture your eye happens to light upon but what is important for you to notice and record. Continuity is *not* an abstract exercise in getting it right. It is not a 'spot the difference in these two pictures' game. It is *what* you notice that is important. You will never notice everything that is happening within a shot and it is not necessary that you should, providing the things you *do* notice and write down are those which are important in order to preserve continuity shot by shot and scene by scene.

Spot the difference
No two people retain an identical impression of a scene or event. Note the differences in the above pictures, which represent two eye-witness accounts of the same accident.

55

Continuity: a Team Effort?

There is the feeling, certainly within television, that continuity is very much a team effort. The costume designer, for example, would therefore be responsible for costume continuity, the props man for action props and so on. Two dangers are inherent in this idea:

Firstly, it is confusing the planning of a production with the shooting. For example, during the planning the costume designer has noted that Scenes 1–4 had direct continuity, and decides that the old tramp appearing in each scene should wear a coat, tied at the waist with string, and a battered hat. When you come to shoot Scene 2, the first in shooting order, the director decides that the hat and coat should be left behind on a park bench. When Scenes 3 and 4 are therefore shot, later in the shooting schedule, the tramp must be without his coat and hat.

But supposing the costume designer was not able to attend the shooting of Scene 2? There might have been a costume fitting to supervise or another urgent appointment. It is also possible that there was not room for all the crew to be present at the shooting due to lack of space.

This is not to denigrate the planning done by the different departments in any way. A great deal of help and assistance are given to continuity by the different members of the unit. But your concern is not with what was planned but what was *actually* shot, scene by scene and day by day.

The second danger is that everyone sees things differently from their own particular interest in the production. Costume will notice costume details to the exclusion of all else, Props will notice props, the cameraman will note the composition and framing of the shot, etc. You are the only person whose responsibility is not to any specific aspect of the shot but to the overall picture, and your concern is how that shot *in its entirety* relates to others *in story order*. You are objective, standing in, in a sense, for the editor and the viewer. You look at all the ingredients that make up the composition of a shot and decide which should have priority over others.

'Costume will notice details to the exclusion of all else'.

Your Role Within the Unit

Avoid being sidetracked

Never be sidetracked into doing anything else when shooting is in progress. Your job is to be where the action is, literally. Continuity implicitly requires you to be there and give your constant attention *all* the time. This does not apply in the feature industry where the job of continuity girl is clearly defined, but in television you must be clear about your role, as so many other aspects are involved.

Never leave the set and always try to be in a position where you can clearly see all the action. This is usually possible even if it means crouching under the camera.

Continuity is your responsibility

You will find during your first day that everyone knows about continuity. The camera opeator says the glass was filled to the brim and positioned on the table. The second assistant insists that the glass was only half full and positioned on the other side of the table. The designer asserts that he left the glass empty on the sideboard and the first assistant swears that there was no glass at all. You *know* that the glass was actually full and in the actor's hand at the relevant moment. (The actor, by the way, remains uncommitted.)

That kind of situation must be stopped before long and involved discussions take place. That is not to imply in any way that no one other than you can be correct about points of continuity. But you are in the unique position of having nothing to do other than watch the action, and if you cannot be more accurate than, say, the second assistant, who might have spent the greater part of the shot stuck behind a bush waiting to give an artist his cue, then you really should not be doing the job.

So do not be perturbed when well-meaning members of the crew come up to you and say, 'Didn't you notice that Fanny's wig was askew during that take?' so long as you *know* that a close-up of Fanny's left foot was being shot.

Always watch the action
Continuity is your responsibility.
Don't ever be sidetracked when
shooting is taking place.

Always try to be in a position
where you can see all the action
even if it means crouching under the camera.

Making Mistakes

You will of course make mistakes. But a large part of the job is that of having confidence in your accuracy, because then you can get the confidence of the unit and time wasting arguments do not arise.

What to do over a mistake

If you or an artiste makes a mistake, and you are immediately aware of it, you can always quietly tell the director and ask for a re-take. Occasionally a director will not re-take for continuity. In that case there is little you can do, except take the rather drastic and ill-advised action of walking into shot, smiling broadly and saying 'Hello Ma'. But after such action you might well find yourself off the set and possibly off the shoot.

If you make an error in a scene already shot and the continuity will affect another scene there are numerous ways of getting round the problem of matching the two scenes. The dialogue could be slightly altered, the first shot for the next scene changed, or even, as happened on the first film I worked on, a new scene written in to overcome a costume error.

Be positive

Always be positive when asked a question. Never fumble through your papers before saying hesitantly: 'Well, I *think* it was with the left hand . . . but of course it might have been the right. . . .' That kind of reply is more irritating than helpful. If you really do not know the answer, say so, positively.

Re-takes for continuity
Except for walking into shot and ruining the take there is little you can do if a director
will not re-take for continuity. In such a situation all you *can* do is point out the
necessity for a re-take and then keep quiet.

Knowledge of the Script

If you have a script it is very important to know it thoroughly before shooting. You should know, for example, where the scene you are about to shoot occurs in the story and whether it has continuity with scenes before or after. Sometimes scenes occur which do not relate to others. Then your job is easier.

Marking up script

Read through the script for continuity, marking important junctions before shooting, so that you will be prepared in advance. Stage directions, entering and exiting, the substitution of stunt artistes in place of the characters and vice versa are all worth noting, as are points in the script which are obvious indications for a change of angle.

Take this piece of dialogue, for example: '*You think this pen is an ordinary one. But, when I remove the top, and unscrew the base, you will appreciate that it is an ingenious weapon.*' I would use a highlighter pen to mark this dialogue, as the director is quite likely to use a cutaway close-up of the pen at that point.

Keep up to date

By doing a little homework each night, while shooting is taking place, you can keep comfortably up to date with continuity. For example, Scene 4 has direct continuity with Scene 5 in that, let us say, two characters are shown in both scenes and there is no time gap. Today you completed shooting Scene 4. Scene 5 will not be shot for another fortnight. If, at the end of today, you sit down with the script and mark in pencil any continuity notes at the top of Scene 5, i.e. '*John and Jill must enter frame right. John wearing blue sweater, green jeans and carrying suitcase in left hand. Jill wearing red/white jacket, blue jeans, red/blue striped blouse (two buttons open at neck) and carrying shoulder bag right shoulder*', then, in two weeks' time, when you come to shoot Scene 5, you will have all the information at your fingertips and not have to scrabble about in the script in order to find the answers to the questions asked by the director.

Script interleaved with notes

The system I use is to carry the script with me, in story order, with the pages of continuity notes of the scenes already shot interleaved with the script pages. Likewise, I would keep any photographs of costume or props together with the script pages for that scene. That makes it easy to check on any continuity queries I might have, as all the relevant notes are together in one file.

Work out a fast reference system

Work out your own system to enable you to check continuity points quickly from scene to scene.

When shooting the second scene (shown above as the second picture) you must be able to check the important points quickly—how the lady is dressed and which way she should enter frame.

Coverage Planned

After getting to know the script, try to find out the director's plans for coverage of a scene.

Important junctions
If you know where the important junctions for cuts will be, you can pay particular attention to the continuity at those points.

The director, of course, may not have any plans, except, one assumes, in his head.

Circulated shot lists
Almost every director I have worked with has started shooting in an incredibly efficient way by having lists of their proposed shots circulated to the unit. After a few days the unit thank you profusely for these lists, fold them up neatly and put them away 'in a safe place', never to be looked at again, and the director then confines his lists to himself and you.

After two weeks or so, even these lists, which have become vaguer day by day, cease, and you must find other ways of determining what sort of shot is being planned.

Shooting script
There are occasions, however, when you might find yourself working for a very well organised director, one who plans well in advance exactly what he is going to shoot and works out each angle with meticulous care. You should of course, think yourself very lucky to be working for such a paragon—but do watch out for one thing.

Such a script can be of immense help in giving a very good idea of what the director *intends* to do, but do beware of following it too slavishly as it may well differ quite considerably from what he *actually* does on the day of shooting. Your job is to note down what actually happened and not what your director's intentions were some five weeks or even five days before the shooting.

Storyboard
Some directors work out a storyboard—sometimes with the help of the graphics designer. A storyboard plots out the story in picture form, showing all the different angles the director plans to shoot. It is a very useful tool as everyone can instantly understand a picture, even if it is just a very simple line drawing, whereas some people might find it harder to visualise a written shot description. The storyboard is used extensively in planning commercials.

The director's plans
There are a number of ways of finding out how the director plans to cover the script.

How to Keep Informed

Stick by the director
At some point the director must communicate with the cameraman, so if you have no idea what shot is to be taken, keep close to the director and cameraman and you will find out.

Master shot then cutaways
Frequently the first shot that is taken in a scene will be some kind of master or establishing shot and the rest of the coverage will follow. But there are no hard-and-fast rules determining how a director will shoot any particular scene.

Position of the zoom handle
When shooting on film, the camera operator may be using a zoom lens by which he can adjust the magnification of the picture or, in other words, the amount of the scene that is included in the shot. Provided the lens is manually operated by a handle, you can judge the size of the shot by the position of the handle. But do find out first whether the wide-angle setting is at the top or bottom of the lens, as they vary. Video cameras have a motorised zoom.

Video monitor
When shooting on video there is the possibility of a monitor on the set. When shooting on film there might also be a separate video monitor attached to the camera.

Keep close behind the camera
Always stand as close to the camera as possible. You cannot describe a shot accurately if you are looking at the scene from a different angle from the camera. Do not set yourself up with a folding table and camp stool some way away from the shooting. You may be comfortable but your notes will be wildly inaccurate.

Look through the viewfinder
No cameraman should object if you ask to look through the camera viewfinder during a rehearsal, provide you chose an opportune moment.

Always ask
Finally, if all else fails, you can always ask the director or the cameraman.

Keep close to the camera
By keeping as near the director and cameraman as possible you not only keep abreast of what angles are being discussed and taken, but are also in a position to describe the shots more accurately.

How to Describe Shots

An accurate shot description is the first essential of continuity. Always describe the shot from the camera's viewpoint (which is also your viewpoint and that of the audience). For example, '*Fred enters frame camera left and exits bottom of frame right*'.

The following gives a list of the most commonly used shot descriptions and abbreviations:

W/A	Wide-angle shot. Such a shot takes place in a wide area of the set in front of the camera. It is sometimes referred to as a VLS (very long shot).
LS	Long shot. A shot which directs the viewer's eye to the depth rather than the width of the shot.
MLS	Medium long shot. Refers to a shot comprising the head to just below the knee of the subject.
3-s	Three shot. A shot containing three central characters.
2-s	Two shot. A shot containing two central characters.
2-s fav. X	A shot with two people—the camera favours one person more than the other.
o/s 2-s	Over the shoulder two shot. Two people are seen in the shot but the camera is looking at one of them over the shoulder of the other.
Mid 2-s	Comprising the head to just below the waist of two people.
Close 2-s	Comprising the head and shoulders of two people.
MS	Mid shot. A scene at normal viewing distance. In the case of a human subject the camera frame cuts the figure just below the waist.
MCU	Medium close-up. The camera frame cuts the figures at chest level.
CU	Close-up. The camera frame cuts the subject just below the neck.
BCU	Big close-up. The face fills the frame.
X's POV	X's point-of-view shot. The camera is X and sees as if from his point of view.
H/A	High angle. The camera is above the action and looking down on it.
L/A	Low angle. The camera is below the action and looking up.

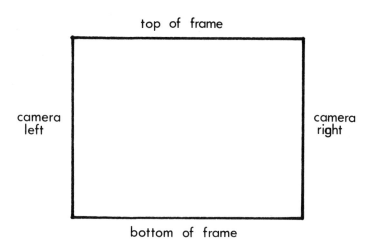

top of frame

camera
left

camera
right

bottom of frame

Exits and entrances

A point to remember is that when referring to entrances and exits always do so from your (also the camera and audience) viewpoint.

Other Terms Used

Camera Movements

PANNING	Camera turns from one side to the other, pivoting horizontally on an axis, either right to left or left to right.
TILTING	Camera pivoting vertically on an axis, tilting up or down.
TRACKING	Camera is physically moved forward or back, towards or away from the subject.
CRABBING	The camera is physiclly moved crab-wise or sideways to the direction of view.
CRANING AND JIBBING	A movement by a camera mounted on a crane dolly. The dolly has a jib arm which can be raised and lowered rotating around its fulcrum.
Z/I	Zoom in. The camera is not moved but the focal length of the zoom lens is increased. This magnifies the subject without changing the perspective of the scene (as opposed to a track where the camera moves towards the subject and the perspective changes as if you were walking towards it).
Z/O	Zoom out. The lens is adjusted in the reverse direction from the above.

Abbreviations relating to action

A/B	As before
FAV	Favouring
F/G	Foreground
B/G	Background
F/WD	Forward
B/WD	Backward
X's	Crosses or across
CAM R	Camera right, i.e. as seen from the camera's—and the viewer's—position when facing the action
CAM L	Camera left
O/S	Over the shoulder
OOV	Out of vision
OOFL(R)	Out of frame (left or right)

Abbreviations relating to sound

MUTE	Without sound
SYNC	Sound recorded synchronously with picture
W/T	Wildtrack (sound recorded without picture)
V/O	Voice-over
MIC	Microphone
GRAMS	Music or sound effects from gramophone records. It is also used as an instruction to the person known as the 'grams operator', therefore, it could also refer to music or sound effects on tape.
TAPE	Music or sound effects solely from tape recordings
F/X	Effects
ATMOS	Atmosphere

70

Description of shots

1. Wide angle (W/A). 2. Long shot (LS). 3. Three shot (3-s). 4. Two shot (2-s). 5. Two shot favouring X (2-s fav. X). 6. Over the shoulder two shot favouring Y (o/s 2-s fav. Y). 7. Mid shot (MS). 8. Medium close-up (MCU). 9. Close-up (CU). 10. Big close-up (BCU). 11. High angle (H/A). 12. Low angle (L/A). 13. Tracking (the camera is mounted on a dolly and physically moved). 14. Panning (the camera turns from one side to the other). 15. Tilting (the camera moves up and down).

Other Terms in General Use

C/A (Cutaway)
This can apply to any shot that is not a master; for example, a close up. Such a shot often emphasises or highlights a particular aspect of events when it is inserted in the main action.

Safety measure
Cutaways are also used as a safety measure. For example: a woman is telling a long story. Several cutaway shots are taken of her audience. The woman's story can then either be shortened by cutting away to the audience, or the cutaways can be used for dramatic effect—to build up atmosphere, heighten tension and generally give pace to a scene.

Under- and over-cranking
On TV, film is shot and projected at a standard rate of 25 frames per second (feature films are projected at 24 fps). That is to say, 25 separate little pictures pass in succession to give the illusion of movement. Any departure from this standard speed in either shooting or projecting the film alters the rate of the action. Under-cranking is a term to denote shooting at less than the standard projection speed; over-cranking for greater than that speed. The 'cranking' part of the term originates from the days when cameras were cranked by hand. Under-cranking and projecting at the normal rate speeds up the action whereas over-cranking slows it down on projection. If a car moving at 30 mph is filmed by under-cranking at 12 fps, (i.e. roughly half the normal rate) it will appear on the screen to be moving at just over 60 mph. If, on the other hand the camera is over-cranking at 50 fps on projection, the car will appear to travel at only 15 mph. (This is impossible with sync sound shots.)

Matte shot
This is a shot in which a mask is inserted in the camera to achieve a particular effect blanking out a part of the picture at the time of shooting, such as in the shape of keyholes, binoculars etc.

Overlay shot
This is filmed material taken for use in a subsequent filming or studio operation, and not containing the complete action. An overlay shot is used later in an electronic studio with action taking place around it, i.e. the countryside passing the windows of a car might be filmed on location and the car and the actors set up in the studio. The live action and the projected background image are then combined in the shot.

BP shot
A BP (or back projection) shot is used in the same way except that the final result is filmed rather than electronically recorded. BP is always shot on 35 mm film material.

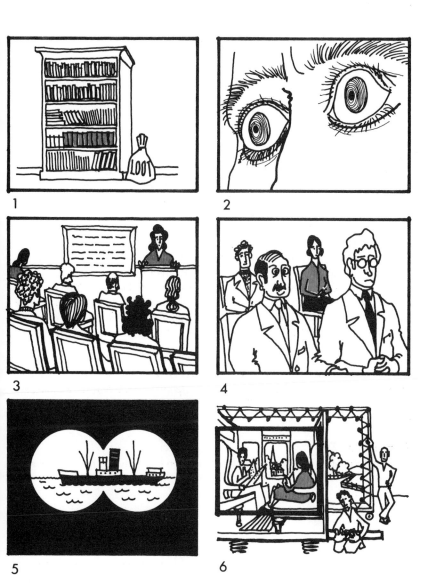

Other terms used

1. Cutaway from W/A of guilty man looking towards bookcase. 2. Cutaway from a close up of a woman screaming. 3. A woman is talking to an audience ... 4. ... a cutaway is taken of the audience to use: (a) to shorten the woman's chat. (b) for dramatic effect. 5. A matte gives a particular effect, e.g.: binoculars. 6. A set using back projection.

Know What to Observe: 1

Good continuity is not *just* being good at observation. It is knowing what is important to observe.

Once you know what the shot is you can observe as necessary.

Close shots

It really is rather a wasted exercise giving detailed information about the clothes an actor is wearing when a large close-up of the face is being shot. It is also unnecessary to worry too much about the position of the props in such a close-up, unless the props are in frame or brought into frame, i.e. a close-up of someone drinking or a cigarette being brought up to the lips.

Mid shots

Be aware of *exactly* what is in shot. For example, someone is reading a book and turning the pages over frequently. In a close-up, all you see is a face, frowning with concentration; in a wide shot you see the whole action with the book in shot. In a mid shot, even though the book itself is not visible do not ignore the operation of turning over the pages, because the upper arm and shoulder movements will be noticeable.

Wide shots

In a very wide shot, it isn't necessary to be as observant of the minute details of actions and props as in the closer shots. In a wide shot of a pub interior with many actors sitting and standing with their drinks, the exact levels of the drink are unimportant, as long as something is in their glasses.

Very long shots

In a very long shot it might prove to be immaterial whether or not there is any drink at all, as it is impossible even to see the glass.

Size of shot

 A

 B

Close shots
Only worry about the clothes or props when these are in frame (A, B).

 C

 D

Mid shots
It is important to know exactly what is in shot. All you see in the close-up is the face (C). In the wide shot you see all the action (D). In the mid shot you will see the upper arm movement as the pages are turned over (E).

 E

 F

Wide shots
You do not have to be as observant of the minute details in this busy station shot (F).

 G

 H

Very long shot
In this long shot it is just possible to see the three figures—let alone details of clothing and props (G, H).

Know What to Observe: 2

It is generally true to say that the more that is happening in a shot, the less continuity matters. But in a constrained, intimate situation, every head turn counts.

Intimate situations

Two characters are having a quiet *tête-à-tête* over dinner. They are eating, and sometimes talking, but nothing much is happening visually. In such a situation it is most important to be accurate about all the actions, even head nods and slight gestures, particularly where the director has planned to cover the scene with complementary two shots. In these shots both characters are in vision all the time and it is only possible to cut from one to the other when the dialogue and action match exactly on each shot.

If the director has planned a coverage of single shots on each person, the action is not so critical as most of it is out of view. The props also are of great importance in such a scene.

The opposite extreme to an intimate situation in terms of observing detail for continuity would be a fight sequence, including a large number of people and props. It would be impossible to notice everything, especially head nods, in a situation with such violent activity. But in this kind of set up you should note carefully what the principal actors are doing and try to keep track of their relationship with other groups.

For instance, in the early part of a scene two principals may be fighting with each other in the thick of other extras. In the latter part of the same scene the principles are still fighting it out, but the extras have cleared save for a group on camera right. So remember that.

Also, be aware of clothes becoming disarranged during a fight and possible make-up requirements, like blood and bruising, that may have continuity with other shots and scenes.

1. In a scene with little action, every detail of continuity is important.

These two complementary 2-shots will only cut together if continuity matches exactly in every detail.

2. But in a scene with a lot of action, accuracy over every detail is not so vital.

Just pay attention to the principal characters and have a general ideal what else is happening in the shot.

Priorities

As you cannot notice *everything* that happens in a shot, what should you concentrate on? Below are a few guidelines:

Largest moving object
The largest moving object within the framework of a shot is the most important to observe as the viewer's attention will be drawn to it—whether it is a head seen in close-up, a person seen in mid shot or a large pink elephant entering frame and dominating the wide shot.

The main characters
If there is a great deal happening in the shot then you should concentrate on the main characters. Stick to watching the people the production is about, who will hold the audience's interest and attention. Others in the shot only assume importance *in relation to* the main characters.

The person speaking
Let us suppose you are doing continuity on a scene containing six principal actors. They are sitting round a table, talking, eating and drinking. How can you possibly notice what they are all doing at any one time? The answer is quite simply that you cannot. But if you ensure that each time the scene is repeated all the props are reset correctly, then the actors will repeat their actions at more or less the same time. Another point to note is that an actor is unlikely to take a bite of a ham sandwich before launching into a speech. But most importantly, you should watch the actor who is talking because the shot used will be more likely to favour the one who is speaking. That is, of course, until the large pink elephant walks into shot!

Bright colours
Bright colours attract the eye, especially if surrounded by drab ones. So notice any areas of bright colour in the shot.

Shots travel in and up
The most interesting part of anyone is the head—unless you are working on a shoe commercial! Coverage of a scene tends, therefore, to travel from the wide shots to the close-ups—inwards and upwards. Thus it is more important to notice the upper part of the body than the lower part and to observe head and arm movements in preference to props littering a table.

'The largest moving object within framework of a shot is the most important to observe as a viewer's attention will be drawn to it . . .'

Props

Ask anyone not connected with shooting—and a good many people who are—what they immediately think of when the term 'continuity' is mentioned. Many believe it is a question of avoiding an accidental total change of costume from one shot to the next, or props appearing in different places from shot to shot, or things suddenly disappearing ... and so on.

There is a good deal more to continuity than maintaining consistency in costume and props, but those are often the most noticeable.

Dressing props
Dressing props are those used to dress the set but are not handled by the actors. Take a Polaroid picture of the set or draw a diagram. This is useful if you are working for several days on the same set or for reference in the case of a shot being retaken.

Action props
Action props are those used by the artistes in the course of the action of a scene. It is most important that you pay particular attention to these props: when the artiste uses them, which hand they are held in and at precisely what point in the dialogue these actions occur.

Resetting props
It the action props are reset in exactly the same way then the artistes will integrate their use with the dialogue and they will be used in the same way and at the same time in the scene. If the props are reset in different positions, the artistes will not get used to handling them and the timing of the actions in relation to the dialogue will be different.

Note the general position of the props by drawing a diagram or taking a Polaroid photograph, but only worry about the props that will be used in the action.

Costume

More arguments and problems seem to arise over costume than almost anything else, but it is really only a matter of working things out intelligently in advance.

The costume designer will have worked out which scenes have continuity of costume with which. But things often happen in the course of the shooting which might bring about changes in the costume in a later scene. For example, an actor might take off his coat in the middle of one scene, and that scene has continuity with another one. Only you would be aware of these points.

Take a Polaroid
At the start of shooting, line all your artistes up and take Polaroid shots of them. Likewise, when they change into another costume.

Write it down
Aways write down exactly what the artiste is wearing at the start of every new scene, and if there is any change within a scene. It might seem tedious, but it will prove its worth at least once within the first week of shooting.

Do not just write down the bare minimum: 'Mrs Bold: hat, coat, dress' does not convey very much information. Is the coat done up or undone? How far is it done up—all the way? What sort of dress is she wearing? What colour? Is her hat on her head or in her hand? What about her shoes? Does she have any accessories like handbag, gloves etc?

My first continuity error was over a scarf that was being worn in one scene and not in the next. My second was over a pair of wellington boots. No one may notice these mistakes, or they might achieve unwelcome fame. With a little care and trouble you need never make them.

Checking
Having taken photographs and made extensive notes, then *use* this information to check when matching continuity of costume.

Make a note or take a Polaroid photograph of costume. You can easily mislay a few items of clothing—especially with period costume.

Not only has the soldier lost his hat—he has also lost his bag, his sword, and the top of his bayonet. It's obvious when the pictures are placed together as these are, but you could easily make the same mistake in the real situation and you had not made copious notes or taken a photograph.

Continuity of Action

Some of the least obvious aspects of continuity are no less important than those already discussed. But they are often overlooked because they are not often apparent in the finished production. The reason they are not apparent is usually because the editor has found a way round the mistakes in one way or another, but in doing so, the artistic role of the post production editing process may have been severely limited. Such errors put an unnecessary and time-consuming burden on the editor.

Let us examine these aspects of continuity by starting with the simplest—continuity of action.

Example 1: A girl walks across a bridge, putting her coat on in the process.

The director has planned two camera angles on this action: one from the bank, with the girl walking away from the camera, and the other from the opposite bank, with the girl walking towards the camera. The cut from one camera angle to the other takes place when the girl is somewhere on the bridge.

Suppose in shooting these two angles, there was an error of continuity in the action of putting on the coat. When the girl put on the coat in the second shot, she was in a different position on the bridge from when she did this in the first shot.

If those shots were then cut and joined together at the logical place, where the director had planned it, the result would show a jump in the action—a jump cut.

It is possible in that situation for the editor to 'cover up' this error of continuity by cutting earlier or later. But that would not give as smooth a cut as if the action had been repeated correctly in the second shot. In other words, the cut had to be made where it was mechanically possible and not in the way that was most suitable dramatically.

Example 2: A man opens a door with a key. He enters and closes the door behind him.

There are two camera angles—one on each side of the door. The second angle is taken much later and as the action with the key has been shot on the first angle, the door is set for the man to just push it open for the second shot. On that angle he pushes the door open and walks in and everyone accepts the take. *But he uses a different hand on the door* and the editor is faced with the same problem as before.

A

B

1st angle

2nd angle
Note that the coat is put on in
a different place in the bridge.
It would not cut together with
the first angle

This would have been the correct
place for putting the coat on

C

D

E

1st angle
Man approaches door (outside)
(D).

F

2nd angle
From the other side of the door
(inside) (E, F).
Continuity of the hands differs
from the first angle. These shots
would not cut together

The position of the hands are
correct in this shot (G)

G

85

Continuity of Action and Dialogue

What happens when there is dialogue as well?

Example 1: A presenter of a programme is coming to the end of a long piece spoken 'to camera'. He moves off, out of frame *after* saying 'We pass on to the next exhibit'. The second angle is a wide exit shot, and he repeats the end of his piece and then moves off. But he starts to move off *on* the words 'We pass on . . .'.

If those two shots were cut together there would either be a loss of action (a jump cut), or double dialogue: 'We pass on' on the first angle, and again 'We pass on' repeated on the second angle.

In such a case the editor would either use the ugly jump cut, or stay on one shot only. He obviously cannot repeat the dialogue. Either way it spoils the intended effect and, if only one shot is used, makes the shooting of the second shot totally pointless. One often sees that a jump cut has been used to get over this type of error. But it is quite wrong to force the editor into using such a jarring effect because of sloppy continuity.

To make the relationship of action to dialogue absolutely clear, take this well-known nursery rhyme:

Example 2: A girl is walking along, swinging a shoulder bag and reciting:
'Mary had a little lamb,
Its fleece was white as snow.
And everywhere that Mary went
The lamb was sure to go.'
On the first angle she places the bag on her shoulder *after* saying: 'Its fleece was white as snow'.

But on the second angle she places the bag on her shoulder *before* saying: 'Its fleece was white as snow'.

When those shots are cut together there is either a sudden jump in the action—from the girl with the bag in her hand, to the girl with the bag on her shoulder, or the action is perfect and the dialogue is as follows:

First angle
'Mary had a little lamb
Its fleece was white as snow'

Second angle
'Its fleece was white as snow,
And everyhere that Mary went
The lamb was sure to go'.

Mary had a little lamb

Its fleece was white as snow

And everywhere that Mary went

The lamb was sure to go.

Action and dialogue

On the first angle the girl places the bag on her shoulder *after* saying 'Its fleece was white as snow' and on the second angle she places it on her shoulder *before* saying the same dialogue.

If those shots are cut together there will either be a jump in the action, or double dialogue.

Drama Situations

It is not often, however, that you have only one character to concentrate on. Things get more complicated as more characters are involved.

Example: A man is sitting on a seat. A girl enters frame—she walks up to the man. She says 'Hello'. The man replies likewise. He gets up and they exit.

That could hardly be simpler. But endless variations of that simple scene are possible.

Does the girl stop *before* she speaks, *as* she speaks, or not at all?

Where does she stop?

When does the man get up?

Does he speak from the seat, on the rise, or standing?

What is the relationship of the man and the girl as she speaks/as he speaks/as he rises?

And so on.

If that simple scene were shot from two angles with both characters in shot in each angle, the continuity has to match exactly on each angle.

first angle   second angle

The simple drama scene
On each angle the action in relation to the dialogue must match exactly, otherwise
the shots 1, 2, 3 will not cut together.

Crossing the Line

Avoiding 'crossing the line' is one of the conventions of single-camera shooting which comes under the umbrella of continuity. The 'line' is an imaginary one, drawn between the noses of two people as they look at each other. Providing the camera does not cross that line, shots that cut directly onto each other will match.

John and Jane are sitting opposite each other. John is on the left of frame and Jane on the right. These positions have been established in the first shot that was taken. Any other shot cutting directly onto or into that shot must feature John on the left and Jane on the right of frame, otherwise it would appear, when the shots are edited together, that the two people have changed places—in other words, they would have jumped from one side of frame to the other.

Single shots

This convention is applicable even to single shots. An interview is being held with the interviewer standing out of shot, to the right of the camera. The interviewee is therefore looking foreground right (to the interviewer). When the shots of the interviewer are taken, he must look foreground left in order that his shot will match that of the interviewee.

Shots that cut directly onto each other

Because this convention only applies to shots that cut directly onto each other the director should work out the coverage of a scene with care, to ensure that when the scene is edited the shots will cut together without crossing the line.

Exceptions

The 'line' can be crossed in the following situations:

1. When the camera moves during the course of a shot, establishing a fresh relationship to the characters;
2. When the characters move, establishing their own different relationship to the camera;
3. When there is a fixed point of reference for the viewer which is unchanged, i.e. a doorway;
4. When the size of shot changes dramatically from one angle to the next.

Both 3 and 4 are known as a 'direct reverse'.

John on
L of frame

Jane on
R of frame

Camera position noted and angle

Dot in a line between people's noses as they look at each other. Providing the camera does not cross that line, shots that cut directly onto each other will match: i.e. John and Jane will remain on the same side of frame as in the original and will not 'jump' in frame.

This direct reverse works. Why? They have their backs to the camera and the bride is on the right. Inside the church the next shot shows them facing the camera. Their positions are reversed.

91

Screen Direction

If an object or person is to appear to travel from destination A to destination B seen in a series of shots of differing angle then it must continue to travel *in the same direction* as has been established in the first shot.

A train is passing through a station. The camera, positioned on Platform 1, sees the train enter frame from the left and exit right. If the camera is then repositioned on Platform 2 it will see the *same train* entering from the right and exiting left. If these two shots were subsequently cut together, the viewer would think either that the train had changed its mind and changed direction or that it was another train.

Our old friend 'crossing the line' is again involved. In this case the direction of movement is the railway track. If the camera crosses the track then the direction of movement appears reversed.

Because the viewer only sees what the camera shows, *from the camera's position in relation to the subject,* there is no external evidence to indicate that the camera itself has changed position, unless this is made apparent in some other way.

Changing direction
Therefore if one has established movement from left to right across the screen this direction must be continued unless:

1. The object changes direction in front of the camera;
2. The camera takes the viewer to a different position by tracking round the moving object;
3. The object travels straight towards the camera or directly away from it;
4. A cutaway is imposed;
5. A shot is taken from within the moving object, i.e. inside the train or car. But beware in this instance of ensuring that the background is moving in the correct direction!

1. The shot of the train taken from Platform 1 and the shot from Platform 2 show the same train apparently travelling in opposite directions.

Drawings and Diagrams

Always draw a quick, rough sketch of each shot. Draw the heads of the characters, denoting their positions in relation to the camera, and their noses, and dot in an imaginary line. Show, in addition, the main props and set dressing. You do not have to be good at art in order to draw a perfectly acceptable diagram. I never progressed beyond stick men at school!

Once you have a diagram of the shot you can use it to match subsequent shots. If you are at any stage confused as to whether the shot about to be taken crosses the line you can show your initial drawing to the director and cameraman, and it will be immensely helpful.

Everyone relates to pictures—that is, after all, the basis of this industry—and it is far easier for you and everyone else to match pictures represented in diagrammatic form rather than try to unravel wordy paragraphs giving the same information.

Note down exits and entrances from the camera's point of view, which is also that of the viewer.

Polaroid cameras

Polaroid cameras are an extremely useful tool for anyone doing continuity, especially for costume and set details, but they are not substitutes for your own simple drawings and notes.

Don't think that by standing beside the film or video camera and taking a picture you will necessarily get a photograph of the same size as is being shot by the cameraman. If you want a close-up photograph of the set dressing on a table go close to the table, possibly stand above it, and then take a picture.

Try to ensure that you have a camera that is in good working order and look after it on location. Don't forget to take plenty of film with you, as it might be hard to obtain in Outer Mongolia!

Always do a rough diagram of the shot, showing the camera position as well as the actors and main props. It does not matter how rough your diagram is, it will be of enormous help in matching future shots.

Rehearsals and Actors

Rehearsals are vitally important as they provide you with your only opportunity of writing down all the information you need. You will never be able to do the job properly if you ignore the rehearsals and only pay attention during the actual take.

There is so much you need to notice in any shot that you can only build up a complete picture bit by bit. Rehearsals afford you the opportunity to do this. For example, during the first rehearsal of a scene, you may not be able to write down the action, but you can at least make a note of the actor's costume. You can also take a Polaroid or other instant picture or draw a diagram of the basic set and the approximate camera position. At the next rehearsal you can note down a bit more—perhaps the overall action, and slowly you will find that you have built up more and more information until you can concentrate entirely on the specific actions and props. Things will be bound to change from one rehearsal to another, but it is far simpler to alter your notes accordingly as and when the changes happen than it is to start writing from scratch during a take.

Problems with actors

If an actor is good with props and naturally does the same action at the same time and with the same bit of dialogue you can stop worrying about him, except to remind him, if requested, of movements when the master shot was taken some time back, or in scenes where the action is complicated.

If an actor is not consistent, watch him or her like a hawk. Don't worry during the rehearsals, but write down the exact movements during a take, so that you can go over them later for cutaways—extra shots of him to be inserted in the main action, if needed. Do not let anyone else tell the actor what he did and when. He will only get confused between your advice and everyone else's. You get in first. It's your job.

The difficult actor

Watch out for the 'difficult' actor. He tends to be terribly nervous and unsure of his actions. He will constantly come up to you to ask anxiously what he did with his left hand in the last take, and will probably worry incessantly about everything. Always have an answer ready. Maybe you did not notice what he did with his left hand. Perhaps it was not even in shot—but never let him know that you have not recorded his every move, in or out of vision. He needs reassurance and will stop worrying only when he feels he can rely on you. You need to keep a careful eye on him for another reason as well; he will argue to the end if he thinks you are wrong about something.

Some actors are good with
props . . .

. . . and some have to be
watched carefully.

Actors and their props

The Complete Scene

We have now looked at the different ingredients to observe for continuity—action, dialogue, props and costume. Now we shall put them all together in the following scene:

Fred and Mabel
Scene 1: Kitchen: day
MABEL IS PREPARING AN APPLE PIE.
FRED COMES IN FROM THE GARDEN AND RUSHES OVER TO THE SINK.
HE TURNS ON THE TAP AND HOLDS HIS HAND UNDER THE STREAM OF WATER.
MABEL GOES OVER TO HIM.

MABEL: Fred, Fred, what's happened?

MABEL EXAMINES HIS HURT HAND.

MABEL: How on earth did you do that?

FRED: The bloody adjuster stuck on the lawn mower.

MABEL: You've got dirt in it.

SHE PUTS HIS HAND BACK UNDER THE TAP.

MABEL: I'll get you a plaster.

SHE GOES TO THE CUPBOARD AND GETS OUT A TIN OF DRESSINGS.

MABEL: Do you want some antiseptic on it?

FRED: No, don't bother.

MABEL TAKES A TOWEL AND GIVES IT TO FRED. HE DRIES HIS HAND ON IT.

FRED: Thanks, love.

MABEL STICKS DRESSING ON FRED'S FINGER. HE WINCES.

MABEL: Did I hurt you?

FRED: No. It's just a bit sore. (PAUSE) Right. I'll finish the lawn.

BOTH GO TO THE BACK DOOR.

FRED: What time's lunch?

MABEL: Is half an hour all right?

FRED: Fine. Give me a shout.

HE KISSES HER AND GOES OUT.

Scene 2: Garden: day
FRED COMES OUT OF THE HOUSE AND WALKS TO LAWN MOWER . . .

The scene is set for Fred and Mabel.

Fred and Mabel: Coverage Planned

The director has planned the following shots for Scene 1 and he has further planned to shoot them in this order:

1. Wide angle of whole scene (master)

2. Tight 2-s Fred and Mabel at sink

3. MCU tap and hand

4. CU dressing going on to finger

5. CU Fred wincing

6. MCU cupboard—tin being removed

7. MS Mabel looking pleased with pie

8. 2-s Fred and Mabel at door

Without being able to show the action in the master shot, I shall try to describe it as fully as possible. When actually doing the continuity for the master, you should have written or noticed as much of the following as possible. There are some obvious pitfalls and important things to notice for the other angles and I have mentioned these where necessary.

Number of shots planned

1. Wide angle (W/A). 2. Tight two shot (Tight 2-s). 3. Medium close-up tap and hand (MCU tap and hand). 4. Close-up plaster (CU plaster). 5. Close-up Fred (CU Fred). 6. Medium close-up cupboard (MCU cupboard). 7. Mid-shot Mabel (MS Mabel). 8. Two shot at door (2-s at door).

Wide Angle: Fred and Mabel Scene: 1

Action and sound

Important to observe

MABEL standing behind the kitchen table puts the last thumb print in the pie and stands back to admire her work.

How does she stand back? Wiping hands on apron or what?

She turns to the oven and opens the door.

Which way does she turn?
Note the oven door action. Is the door left open or shut?

She turns back to table and picks up pie.

FRED comes in through back door (which is closed to start), he leaves it open, crosses behind Mabel and dashes to sink. He turns on the tap with left hand and puts finger of right hand under the jet of water.

Back door closed to start—left open by Fred—keep an eye on it.
Which tap does Fred turn on and with which hand?
Which finger of which hand is cut?

MABEL puts pie back on table— closes door of the oven with her knee in passing and hurries over to Fred.

Pie does not figure again, but it is left on the table so do not forget that it is there.

Note oven door action.

MABEL: Fred, Fred, what's happened?

Does she say that line on the move or when she is by Fred's side?
Which side of Fred does she end up on?

FRED doesn't answer. Just swears under his breath.

MABEL is now at the sink. She takes his right hand with her left.

Which hand takes which? Important to note that the tap is left running.

MABEL: How on earth did you do that?

FRED: The bloody adjuster stuck on the lawn mower.

MABEL: You've got dirt in it.

She sticks his hand back under the tap.

During the above dialogue, does she hold his hand all the time? Does she bring his hand up to her face to look closely at the wound, or bend down to look. When *exactly* does she stick his hand back under the tap?

MABEL: I'll get you a dressing.

She crosses to the cupboard—opens the door (right hand to open it)—takes out tin of dressings (with right hand)—transfers tin to her left and says:

MABEL: Do you want some antiseptic on it?

FRED: No, don't bother.

Note all her actions at the cupboard—which hand does what. N.B. There is a bottle of antiseptic in the cupboard. Make sure it is still there for the cutaways.

Does she say that line while transferring the tin to left hand or after?

Plan view of kitchen with camera position showing complete scene as per page 98.

. . . and continue doing.

Wide Angle: Fred and Mabel Scene: 2

Action and sound	*Important to observe*
MABEL leaves the cupboard door open—moves to the back door—half closes it and with her right hand picks up a towel from a hook on the back.	Note that cupboard door. I said to keep an eye on the back door.
She moves forward to the sink. FRED turns off the tap with his left hand and takes the towel from Mabel also with his left hand.	Tap action. At what point does Fred turn it off? i.e.: what is Mabel doing then? Which hand does he turn it off with and does he take the towel before or after turning off the tap and with which hand?
FRED starts gingerly to dry his cut finger.	
MABEL opens the tin of dressings with her right hand and puts the lid down (upside down) on the draining board.	Note the action—particularly with the lid.
She takes out a dressing and puts the tin down on the draining board beside the lid (on the right side).	
FRED: Thanks love.	When does Fred speak? Is Mabel still taking the lid off the tin, or the dressing out of the tin or what?
FRED throws the towel down on the draining board.	Note that Fred speaks and then throws the towel down. Also note where it lands.
MABEL unpeels the dressing from its backing and places it on Fred's finger. Fred turns his head away and winces.	Does she use both hands to place the dressing on his finger? Note the way Fred's head turns to wince.
MABEL: Did I hurt you?	Note that she speaks before he turns his head back.
FRED turns his head back.	
FRED: No, it's just a bit sore.	
MABEL takes her hands away.	Note when she removes her hands.
FRED: Right. I'll finish the lawn.	

MABEL picks up the towel with her left hand and moves to the door.	Note the hand.
FRED picks up the lid of the dressings tin and places it on the box— picks up the box with left hand and moves to the door.	Note the hand, also that Mabel moved to door before Fred.
MABEL hangs the towel up at the door—FRED moves over to her with the tin which he hands over (his left hand to her right).	Note the hand action.

FRED: What time's lunch?

MABEL: Is half an hour all right?

FRED: Fine. Give me a shout.	Do not forget that during the dialogue Mabel is holding the tin.
FRED kisses her. He pulls open the door and goes out.	Kisses her after the dialogue. Note. You see about the door?

N.B. when you come to do the scene directly following this one, which is Exterior, Garden, you will of course know that Fred must have a dressing on the relevant finger of his right hand, and that the back door is slightly open, at the start of the shot, before Fred comes out!

Remaining Coverage: Fred and Mabel Scene: 1

Having shot the master, the director goes on to shoot the rest of the coverage. This is your first test.

2-s Fred and Mabel at sink
From Fred turning on the tap—putting his hand under the water—you will remember which tap and which hand—Mabel comes up to him—she examines his hand—chat—tap still running—she replaces his hand under the tap—she exits frame (do you know which way?)—chat with her out of vision—she returns with towel and tin (in which hands?)—Fred turns off tap and takes towel—he dries his hand. Mabel meanwhile goes through the same actions as the master shot opening the tin. Fred puts the towel on the draining board. Mabel places dressing on Fred's finger. Fred turns his head away (which way?) and winces. Mabel speaks—Fred turns back to her and speaks—Mabel takes her hand away. Fred says he will finish the lawn. Mabel takes the towel and exits. Fred does his action with the tin of dressing and also exits.

MCU tap and hand
Hand in to tap—turns on water (which tap and which hand?). The finger, (suitably wounded) is placed under the water.

CU dressing going on finger
Mabel's hand holding dressing—places it on Fred's outstretched finger and presses firmly into place. (Make sure that Fred's finger is no longer wet, as he has just dried it with a towel.)

CU Fred wincing
Fred turns his head and winces. Mabel says her line out of vision and Fred turns back.

Other shots planned

Tight two shot (Tight 2-s)

Medium close-up tap
and hand (MCU tap and hand)

Close-up plaster (CU plaster)

Close-up Fred (CU Fred)

Remaining Coverage: Fred and Mabel Scene: 2

MCU cupboard

The cupboard door is shut to start. Mabel's right hand opens the door and reveals a tin of dressings and a bottle of antiseptic (both of which have been replaced after the W/A)—her right hand takes the bottle, then replaces it and takes tin of dressings—the cupboard door is left open and she moves her hand away.

MS Mabel looking pleased with the pie

As you noted on the master that she rubs her hands on the front of her apron, she can repeat that action. You also noted the way she turned to the oven, and that she left the pie on the table and did not take it with her.

2-s Fred and Mabel at door

Mabel goes to back door (holding the towel in left hand). The back door is half closed. She hangs the towel on the back. Fred enters from foreground to form a two-shot (Fred's finger is dressed and he carries the tin with him in his left hand). He hands tin to Mabel—chat—he kisses her and goes out through door.

Summing up

So, what are you left with at the end? First you have the whole scene played in wide angle, with everything contained in the one shot. Then you have a number of other shots from different angles of various sections of the scene. Because you have ensured that the action during every shot is as near as possible identical to the master wide angle, it will be possible to cut, say, from the master of the 2-s of Fred and Mabel at the sink, to the MCU of the taps, and so on at any one of a number of places. The cuts will then be determined in order that each piece of action may be seen in the final result from the most suitable angle in accordance with the dramatic interpretation of the script, and the resulting material available.

Remainder of shots planned

Medium close-up cupboard
(MCU cupboard)

Mid shot Mabel (MS Mabel)

Two shot at door (2-s at door)

Fred and Mabel: Edited Sequence

Finally, the scene has been edited, and the completed sequence might look like this:

Scene 1: Int. Kitchen. Day

1.	W/A	/MABEL IS PREPARING AN
2.	MS Mabel	APPLE PIE/
3.	W/A	FRED COMES IN/FROM THE GARDEN AND RUSHES
4.	MCU tap	OVER TO THE SINK. HE TURNS/ON THE TAP AND HOLDS HIS HAND UNDER THE STREAM OF WATER
5.	2-s at sink	MABEL GOES OVER TO HIM/

MABEL: Fred, Fred, what's happened?

MABEL EXAMINES HIS HAND

MABEL: How on earth did you do that?

FRED: The bloody adjuster stuck on the lawn mower.

MABEL: You've got dirt in it.

SHE PUTS HIS HAND BACK UNDER THE TAP

MABEL: I'll get you a dressing

6.	W/A	SHE/GOES TO THE CUPBOARD AND GETS
7.	MCU cupboard	OUT/A TIN OF DRESSINGS

MABEL: Do you want some antiseptic on it?

8.	W/A	/FRED: No, don't bother.
9.	2-s	MABEL TAKES A TOWEL AND GIVES IT TO FRED./ HE DRIES HIS HAND ON IT.

FRED: Thanks love.

10.	MCU dressing	MABEL STICKS DRESSING/ON FRED'S
11.	Cu Fred	FINGER/HE WINCES
12.	2-s	/MABEL: Did I hurt you?

FRED: No. It's just a bit sore. (PAUSE)

Right. I'll finish the lawn.

13.	2-s by door	BOTH GO/TO BACK DOOR

FRED: What time's lunch?

MABEL: Is half an hour all right?

FRED: Fine. Give me a shout.

14.	W/A	HE KISSES/HER AND GOES OUT.

110

The edited sequence

1. Wide angle
2. Mid shot Mabel
3. Wide angle
4. Medium close-up tap and hand
5. Tight two shot
6. Wide angle
7. Medium close-up cupboard
8. Wide angle
9. Tight two shot
10. Close-up plaster
11. Close-up Fred
12. Tight two shot
13. Two shot at door
14. Wide angle

111

Direct and Indirect Continuity

We have examined the relationship of action, dialogue, props and costume within a scene. Now that scene must be related to others. Two forms of continuity are involved here: direct and indirect continuity.

Direct continuity
Direct continuity means that actions are carried over from one scene to the next with no time lapse. Reverting to the Fred and Mabel scene, there was direct continuity between the end of Scene 1, with Fred walking out of the back door, dressing on his finger, and the start of Scene 2, with Fred coming through the door into the garden, dressing still on his finger. What is important to remember is that these scenes will not be shot consecutively—indeed Scene 2 may well be shot first, therefore accurate notes on the beginnings and endings of scenes are vital.

Indirect continuity
Indirect continuity refers to continuity links between scenes that are not consecutive. It means that there is some sort of break—a time lapse, a scene interposed which deals with other characters or some other aspect of the story, but where there are continuity links between these scenes however spaced out in the story order. These different continuity threads might not be immediately apparent on reading the script or when each individual scene is shot, maybe days or weeks apart.

For example: Scene 1 ends with a man stuffing a package into the right hand pocket of his coat. Scenes 2 and 3 are centred round another character. Scene 4 shows our man from Scene 1 walking along a street to a rendezvous. It must be remembered that he is wearing a coat from Scene 1. Scene 5 shows the man meeting his contact. The man hands over the package. There is therefore indirect continuity with Scene 1, the package in the right hand coat pocket; with Scene 4, wearing the coat; and possibly for the contact with later scenes.

Remember that none of the above are shot in story order, which makes the whole matter more complex.

Knowing the script thoroughly prevents you from being caught unawares by indirect continuity.

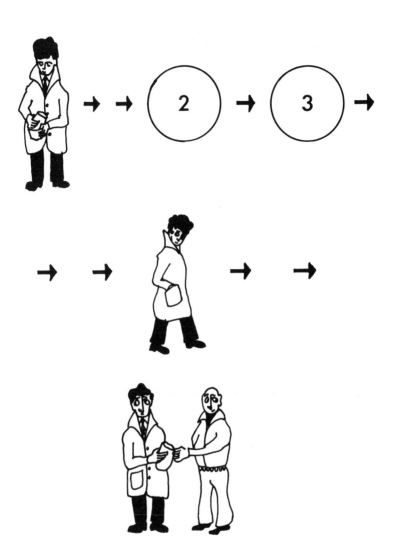

Scenes related to others

Scene 1 ends with the man putting the parcel into his coat pocket

Scenes 2 and 3 are concerned with other things

Scene 4 shows our man from Scene 1 (therefore there is indirect continuity from 1 to 4)

Scene 5 shows the man handing parcel over (therefore there is indirect continuity with Scene 1 and direct continuity from Scene 4)

Matching Continuity

Checking

Once you have established continuity on a shot that has been taken then any shot that, in the final edited version, will cut into or onto that shot will need to match for continuity.

In matching continuity, therefore, you are not so much involved in writing fresh notes but in checking. You check the artistes' costume against your notes and photographs; you check the props against your drawings. You check that the camera angle is not going to cross the line so that objects and people jump in frame. During the rehearsals and the shooting you check the dialogue and that the actors' actions are the same and happen at the same time in relation to the dialogue as the shot already taken. In other words, you are not busy writing down fresh notes, unless there is new material being rehearsed and shot, but you are using those you have already made in order to match continuity.

If an actor gets it wrong

Never go directly to the artiste and point out continuity errors without first speaking to the director. It is discourteous to the director, who is ultimately responsible for accepting the actor's interpretation and performance. The continuity might have been wrong but the performance so stunning that the director might not wish to retake the shot but decides to get round the continuity problem in other ways. There might not be time to retake for continuity or the director might know that the specific continuity error is unimportant. You must always speak to the director first.

If you are then asked to tell the actor, always go up to him or her with the script and explain the problem quietly, showing the actor the script. It is very confusing to the actor if you shout across the set from your position by the camera.

If the director won't listen

There is nothing you can do in the situation where a director won't listen or ignores a point of continuity which you feel to be important, except note on the continuity report sheet that the continuity was wrong. That could prove helpful to the editor.

Which 'take' do you match for continuity?

Let us say you have shot six takes on one particular angle. The director thinks that take 1 is possible and so is take 6. The continuity on those takes differs, and you are about to shoot another shot which has direct continuity with the one just recorded. You ask the director which take he prefers, in order to match continuity. The director will not, or cannot, specify, saying that he will look at both takes in the editing. Do you match continuity to take 1 or take 6?

As the director has not spoken in favour of either take, it is then up to you to decide which to match for continuity. I would always match continuity to the last take (take 6 in this example), as the artistes are far more likely to remember how they performed five minutes ago rather than two hours ago. Also, the last take must have been satisfactory enough for the director to move on to another shot.

'If you are then asked to tell the actor, always go up to him and explain the problem quietly.'

Recording on Videotape: 1

For some reason, people often get confused about the necessity for continuity when recording onto videotape. The past legacy of videotape being thought of solely in terms of a multi-camera studio-based facility remains.

But videotape has, over the past ten years, changed enormously. The advent of small-format (three-quarter and half inch) videotape in cassette form has made a far more mobile and flexible resource than the studio or outside broadcast operation to which it was previously confined. Cameras have become smaller and lighter and receptive to far lower levels of lighting than film. The greatest changes have taken place in the area of videotape editing which, from very primitive beginnings, has progressed to the stage where, for example, very many TV commercials, shot on film, are immediately transferred to videotape and edited electronically.

All this means that there is no hindrance to the flexibility of shooting on videotape using the film-style technique of single-camera, out of sequence shooting, and this system is becoming more and more popular. Once a film-style technique is adopted, however, the need for continuity is there, and the PA should be quite clear about her role.

Scripted

If the material is scripted then the role of continuity is just as important as if shooting on film. Sometimes a slate board will be used, not so much as a means of identification but rather as a discipline to alert the unit that recording is about to commence.

Timecode

The shot is identified by means of the 'in' point of timecode, and this must be noted either on a continuity sheet or a shot list. Timecode is a method whereby each video is identified by means of numbers broken down into hours, minutes, seconds and frames. Each frame always keeps its original identity, known as the timecode address. The timecode recorded onto the tape can either show the tape running time or the actual time of day.

Unscripted

If the material is unscripted then the role of continuity remains the same as for the same type of programmes shot on film. The shot list becomes additionally important, as tape is cheap in comparison to film and directors and cameramen will not stint themselves in the amount they shoot.

Timecode logging
Timecode shown in hours, minutes and seconds.

Recording on Videotape: 2

'Let's play it back . . .'

When recording on videotape, generally there is the immensely useful facility of having a monitor within easy access, making the job of giving an accurate shot description very simple. There is always the facility, in matters of dispute over continuity, of being able to play back the tape. But this facility should be used sparingly, as it wastes time on location and can lead to the general cry of 'Let's play it back' over the smallest query.

Continuity from a central control area

Some productions, while shooting single-camera, will have the recording taking place inside a car, a van or an outside broadcast scanner. In that situation should you remain in the control area during recording or be on the set? Can you do the job of continuity from a distance, while peering at a monitor?

Communication

If you attempt to do the job of continuity from a distance you will undoubtedly have problems with communication. It is very difficult to convey, through a stage manager or second assistant, the exact way in which an artiste picked up a cup. It is far easier and far less time wasting to go and show the artiste yourself.

Continuity from a monitor

It is not easy to do continuity from a monitor. First, the screen is flat, second, it is small, and third, it is only possible for you to view the shot when the cameraman is fully ready, whereas to do the job properly you need to be making notes when the cameraman is still setting up.

Stay with the director

Whatever you opt for, there will be times when you feel that you are in the wrong place. The only sensible course must be to remain with your director, and if he elects to direct from the set, then that is where you should be. But if he decides to direct from the control room, your place is there.

Plus points

There are, of course, advantages to remaining inside a nice warm, dry vehicle while the rest of the unit freezes in a force 10 gale . . . but do make sure that your material comfort is not at the expense of the job . . .

Do you remain in the control room or go out on the set doing the job of continuity? Whichever you opt for, there will be times when you feel that you are in the wrong place.

Working on Documentary-type Productions: 1

You will always know something

Even if you are working on a production that appears to be totally unscripted and unplanned, you will always know *something* before you arrive on location—even if it is only the subject matter.

If, for example, you know nothing more than that you are working on a documentary about drink, then at least you can begin to focus your attention somewhere. Anything liquid, in bottles, restaurants, homes, on tables, in shops, should attract your interest.

Continuity

The job of continuity will, of necessity, be less precise than on scripted productions, but all the points in earlier chapters should be taken into consideration:

Shot description

An accurate and full shot description is of first importance. It is not enough to note simply 'Close-up large machine' without finding out and stating what the object is. This is especially important when the subject matter is of a technical nature. Neither is it sufficient to note 'Close-up of manometer' without giving a description. The editor is extremely unlikely to know what a manometer is and the director may well have forgotten.

Names and addresses

Always note down the names, addresses and titles of those taking part, e.g. *Chairman of Blogswich Cricket Club, 1951*, taking care to ensure that the spelling is accurate. Your note on your shot list may end up on a graphic on the completed programme.

Locations

Always note the location in your shot description. To state:

'W/A mountain

W/A different mountain

GV group of mountains'

is not that helpful to the editor, the director or the person writing the commentary.

'If you're working on a documentary about drink . . . the job of continuity will, of necessity, be less precise.'

Working on Documentary-type Productions: 2

Costume

Costume details should be noted, especially if members of the public, dressed in their own clothes, are involved. If clothes continuity is important, then Mr Bloggs, whose geraniums won first prize at the flower show, must be tactfully asked to wear the same scruffy gardening clothes on three successive days of shooting. Where a presenter is seen in different locations, all shot out of sequence, then continuity of clothes should be carefully worked out and discussed in advance.

Basic continuity

Simple, basic continuity should be observed, such as exits and entrances and moves within a shot. Attention should be paid, as far as possible, to the conventions of single-camera shooting such as the avoidance of crossing the line and screen direction.

If a demonstration is given, with ad lib commentary, then the moves should be noted for subsequent cutaways.

Interviews

When an interview is shot, the questions should be noted down in order to relay them to the interviewee for later shots.

Public relations

One of your main tasks, when shooting, lies in the area of public relations. You may find yourself placating irate gentlemen who are unable to park their cars in their usual place due to the crew vehicles. You might spend hours explaining to members of the public what is going on and why there are lights and cameras. You will need a pocketful of coins to bribe children to go away, and you could find yourself chatting to nervous old ladies who have not had a wink of sleep the previous night, partly in dread of their forthcoming interview and partly for fear of disarranging their expensive hairdo, in a manner quite unlike your usual, rather reticent self.

In short, you act as trouble-shooter, paver of ways and smoother-out of difficulties.

The best advice I can give is to be prepared for anything to happen.

Trouble-shooter
Much of your job during shooting will be that of general factotum, fixer and trouble-shooter. You will smooth the way for an untroubled, fast, efficient shoot, and if anything goes wrong you will be blamed.

123

Writing It Down

The person doing the job of continuity needs to make a lot of notes. These are of use:

1. To yourself and the unit while shooting is taking place, in order to preserve continuity from shot to shot and scene to scene; and
2. To the editor, by providing a written log of the shooting.

Scripted and unscripted

If you are working with a script many of your continuity notes will be written on the script itself, as you will be able to pinpoint actions precisely in relation to the dialogue. You will, in addition, fill in continuity report sheets in order to provide shot-by-shot information. A fresh sheet should be used for every shot. There are various printed sheets available, which vary considerably in design and layout. These can be used when recording either on film or on videotape.

If you are working without a script you will need to provide a detailed shot list. I would use a notebook or larger sheets of ruled paper in order to compile the shot list on location.

How to organise the paperwork

When you are standing in a muddy field with the wind wreaking havoc with your notes and the director asks you whether, in Scene 64, the actor has his coat undone or done up, do you—after inwardly cursing—have to get down on your knees and wrestle with several large files in order to find the answer? How, in other words, do you organise the paperwork you carry with you on location in order to make the job as simple as possible?

Most people develop their own systems, after a certain amount of trial and error, and if you have one which works well for you, then don't consider changing it.

The system I use

I keep the script in a file in story order. I do not have another version of the script in shooting order as my interest is in the continuity between scenes when the material is finally edited together.

Each day I will extract from this file the pages of the scenes we are about to shoot. I put these on a clipboard, on top of blank continuity sheets which are held down by a rubber band. It becomes very easy, then, to work on the script and make notes on the continuity report sheet by flicking from one to the other.

At the end of the day I will replace the pages of script in the file in story order together with my rough continuity sheets and any relevant photographs. In this way, any query about Scene 64 only means looking in one place in one file.

FILM AND VIDEO CONTINUITY NOTES

PRODUCTION		EPISODE	SCENE	SLATE / IDENT
NUMBER DATE				

FILM CAMERA ROLL	FILM SOUND ROLL	VIDEOTAPE REEL NUMBER	(Circle whichever is appropriate)						
			INT.	DAY	NIGHT	SYNC	GUIDETRACK	WILDTRACK	
			EXT (Weather)			MUTE	PLAYBACK		

LOCATION / SHOT DESCRIPTION

CAMERA INFORMATION (If appropriate)
LENS _____
DISTANCE _____
STOP _____
FILTERS _____

TIMECODE OR ENDBOARD	TAKE*	DURATION	REMARKS (Reason if take is NG)	CONTINUITY NOTES (Including costume/props/dialogue/drawings etc.)
	1			
	2			
	3			
	4			
	5			
	6			
	7			
	8			
	9			
	10			

Circle acceptable takes - if more than 10 takes, use second sheet.

125

When You Make Notes

You are standing on the set, by the camera, on the first day of shooting. The world seems to have gone mad around you, with everyone busy rushing round, attending to their own concerns. At what point do you start to do your job and begin taking notes?

Write what you can when you can

You should start to take notes as soon as possible. The order in which things will happen will vary, but you should make it a rule to write down what you can when you can and always be alert to what is going on around you.

If you are working on a production where continuity is of great importance, you should *never* leave the set when shots are being discussed, set up, rehearsed and recorded. You should not retire to a little room, set aside for your purposes, in order to type up yesterday's continuity sheets. If you do, you will not be able to keep up with what is happening today.

Although it would be helpful to watch a rehearsal without taking any notes, you might find that you then don't have enough time to take sufficient notes later on. You will never be able to write down all you want and you should use every second available.

Pens or pencils?

Do you make notes using pencil or coloured pen? There are two options open to you, both with advantages and disadvantages.

First, always take rehearsal notes in pencil. That way, you can alter your notes as things change. If you continue to use pencil when shooting, you should make sure that you can distinguish the different takes, perhaps by writing in 'take 1' and 'take 2' beside the notes. The advantage of continuing to use pencil is that you can erase wrong or altered notes and your script remains fairly clean and legible. The disadvantage lies in being unable to differentiate between rehearsal notes and notes relating to the recording, unless you are very careful.

You will not have this problem if you use coloured pens for your notes when recording. The difficulty with this system lies with the director who shoots a number of takes of each angle. You will need a good colour-code system to remember that pink relates to take 12, and the danger is that your script will become excessively messy and hard to read.

'You should not retire to a little room, set aside for your purpose.'

Continuity Report Sheet: General

Many companies have their own continuity report sheets. The form shown opposite was designed by the author to be used on either film or video shooting.* Let us examine in detail what should be written on a continuity report sheet.

Production details
The first details to be written are the name of the production, the production number and date.

Episode/scene
The episode (if a series) and the scene or sequence number should be marked. A script is divided into scenes—each new location being a new scene. A scene is often called a sequence but, to be strictly accurate, a sequence is the final cut version of the scene. If there is a separate shot number, put that down.

Slate/ident
The slate number relates to material shot on film and is the number given to each photographed shot. It is a means of cataloguing the shot. Almost always the first shot of the first day's shooting is called Slate Number 1 and proceeds consecutively until the last shot of the last day of shooting.

The slate number is shown marked up on a clapperboard at the start of each shot. This board has a twofold purpose. In the days of silent pictures each shot would be identified by the humblest member of the camera department holding up a piece of slate with a number chalked on it. When talkies arrived he would, in addition, bang together two pieces of wood—called a clapstick—to establish synchronisation between action and sound. Later the two were combined to form the clapperboard. The board is still called the 'slate' by tradition and the individual shot itself, being identified by a slate number, is colloquially referred to as 'a slate'.

If shooting on videotape a clapperboard might still be used to identify the shot, although there would be no need to bang together the pieces of wood. In this box, therefore, the shot number should be written. If there is no shot number then the 'in' point of timecode would act as the reference point on the tape for that particular shot.

Interior or exterior
Mark whether you are shooting an interior or an exterior scene and note the weather, if exterior. Just 'dull' or 'sunny' will suffice.

*Supplies available from the author, on (0386) 792 051.

FILM AND VIDEO CONTINUITY NOTES

PRODUCTION		EPISODE	SCENE	SLATE / IDENT
NUMBER	DATE			

FILM CAMERA ROLL	FILM SOUND ROLL	VIDEOTAPE REEL NUMBER	(Circle whichever is appropriate)						
			INT.	DAY	NIGHT	SYNC	GUIDETRACK	WILDTRACK	
			EXT (Weather)			MUTE	PLAYBACK		

LOCATION / SHOT DESCRIPTION

CAMERA INFORMATION (If appropriate)
LENS _____
DISTANCE _____
STOP _____
FILTERS _____

TIMECODE OR ENDBOARD	TAKE*	DURATION	REMARKS (Reason if take is NG)	CONTINUITY NOTES (Including costume/props/dialogue/drawings etc.)
	1			
	2			
	3			
	4			
	5			
	6			
	7			
	8			
	9			
	10			

* Circle acceptable takes - if more than 10 takes, use second sheet.

© Avril Rowlands 1989

129

Continuity Report Sheet: Technical

Roll numbers

Note down the camera and sound roll numbers if shooting on film. If shooting on videotape, note the tape reel number.

Sound

If shooting on film, the next thing to note down relates to sound. Is the shot taken sync—that is, with camera and sound 'locked' together and running synchronously? Or is it to be a silent or 'mute' shot (with no sound recording being made)? If the sound is being recorded by itself without shooting a picture, this is known as a 'wild track', sometimes written as 'wildtrack'. The expression 'wildtrack with camera' means that the sound is recorded simultaneously with the shooting of the picture but with no interlock between camera and recorder. All under- and over-cranked shots which have sound recorded for them at the same time fall into this category.

'Guidetrack' indicates that the camera and sound are running in sync: the sound is intended only as a guide to the editor and is not of good enough quality to be used in the completed film. 'Playback' is the term used when pre-recorded music is played into the shot in order that the actors can time their actions correctly from one shot to another.

Camera information

This information is sometimes given to you to write down, but only when shooting on film. Ask the cameraman whether it would be helpful to note the following or not.

Lens

A film camera can be equipped with one or more zoom lens or a set of fixed focal length ones, which are often referred to as 'prime' lenses. Details of the lens that is being used for each particular shot would be given to you to note down.

Distance

This refers to the measured distance between the camera and the subject. This can be measured by eye, focusing through the viewfinder, or by using a tape measure and setting the distance on the lens scale.

Stop

The cameraman will take a light reading from his exposure meter, having first adjusted the meter for the type of film used. From that reading, a number is obtained, which is known as the 'F' or 'T' stop. ('F' means Focal, and 'T' means Transmission.) This stop is then set on the lens iris, thus controlling the amount of light passing through the lens.

Special filters

Film stock is balanced for a certain light intensity, and most film is balanced for artificial (tungsten) light. If filming in daylight, therefore, the cameraman normally needs to compensate by using an orange filter (a wratten 85). This is the most common one used. Other widely used filters are of neutral density (ND), which reduce the light intensity but do not change the colour temperature. There are many other filters that can be used to create different effects and details of these would be given to you by the cameraman.

FILM AND VIDEO CONTINUITY NOTES

PRODUCTION Lost Days in Atlanta		EPISODE	SCENE	SLATE / IDENT
		4	34	68

NUMBER ZT/1039/Y	DATE 30·4·89

FILM CAMERA ROLL	FILM SOUND ROLL	VIDEOTAPE REEL NUMBER	(Circle whichever is appropriate)				
			INT. (DAY) NIGHT	(SYNC)	GUIDETRACK		WILDTRACK
12	20		(EXT) Overcast, rain (Weather)	MUTE	PLAYBACK		

LOCATION / SHOT DESCRIPTION	CAMERA INFORMATION (If appropriate)
	LENS 25 mm
	DISTANCE 12 ft
	STOP 3·5
	FILTERS 85

TIMECODE OR ENDBOARD	TAKE*	DURATION	REMARKS (Reason if take is NG)	CONTINUITY NOTES (Including costume/props/dialogue/drawings etc.)
	1			
	2			
	3			
	4			
	5			
	6			
	7			
	8			
	9			
	10			

* Circle acceptable takes - if more than 10 takes, use second sheet.

© Avril Rowlands 1989

131

Continuity Report Sheet: Continuity

Next you write down the notes that are specifically for continuity.

Location
You should note the location, either by writing 'The Happy Haymaker's Pub, Grove Road, Dorset', or just 'pub'. It all depends on whether there is a separate list of locations on the schedule and how important you feel the information to be.

Shot description
This description should state how a shot begins, how it ends and any development in the middle. It should be as concise as possible and an easy reference for yourself or the editor.

Continuity notes
The space on the right of the sheet is left blank for you to fill in information which is important for continuity.

At the start of a new scene always write what the artistes are wearing and how their hair is arranged. Make a note of any props they are carrying, e.g. a walking stick. Notes about make-up are only made for a major effect, like a cut cheek, which would heal during the progress of the story.

You might use the space to note any specific dressing props, 'N.B. Fire must be alight', and you should make a sketch of the shot, with the position of the camera and actors noted down. You might also draw diagrams of set dressing—for example, a table laid for a meal.

Either note down the 'in' and 'out' words of dialogue or mark the coverage on your script. It is very important to know where in the scene the shot begins and ends.

FILM AND VIDEO CONTINUITY NOTES

PRODUCTION			EPISODE	SCENE	SLATE / IDENT
LOST DAYS IN ATLANTA			4	34	68
NUMBER 2T/1039/Y	DATE 30·4·89				

FILM CAMERA ROLL	FILM SOUND ROLL	VIDEOTAPE REEL NUMBER	(Circle whichever is appropriate)		
12	20		INT. (DAY) NIGHT	(SYNC) GUIDETRACK	WILDTRACK
			(EXT) Overcast, rain (Weather)	MUTE PLAYBACK	

LOCATION / SHOT DESCRIPTION

HIGH STREET

2-s Mr. Mrs Jones → they exit R at end

CAMERA INFORMATION (If appropriate)	
LENS	25mm
DISTANCE	12 ft
STOP	3·5
FILTERS	85

TIMECODE OR ENDBOARD	TAKE*	DURATION	REMARKS (Reason if take is NG)	CONTINUITY NOTES (Including costume/props/dialogue/drawings etc.)
	1			from: start of scene to: "it really is too bad" (BOTH EXIT)
	2			Mr J: black suit, jacket undone,
	3			red waistcoat, white shirt, red/white spotted cravat, hat r. hand / walking stick L. hand,
	4			Mrs J: green/grey striped dress, shawl (grey)
	5			over shoulders. Hair tied back in bun. Basket r. hand.
	6			
	7			
	8			
	9			
	10			

* Circle acceptable takes - if more than 10 takes, use second sheet.

© Avril Rowlands 1989

133

Continuity Report Sheet: Details of Shooting

The information on the left-hand side of the sheet relates to the shooting and is of vital importance to the editor.

E/B or T/Code

An endboard usually relates to shooting on film and refers to the clapperboard. Sometimes the board is not put on the front of the shot but at the end—for example, when something should be filmed instantly and without the delay of putting a board in front of the camera. The board is held upside down to indicate to the editor that it refers to the shot that has just ended.

A timecode reference should be used against each take when shooting on videotape. Either the 'in' timecode of this take or the 'out' point of the preceding one should be shown.

Takes

A take is the recording of the action of a shot. If that action is not satisfactory for some reason the same action is repeated using the same slate number (if shooting on film) or shot number, but identified as 'take 2'. If that is not satisfactory either, there is another take, and so on until the director is satisfied.

On your continuity sheets you should circle the accepted takes. The others are marked NG (No good). But you should always give a reason *why* a take is NG. This is most important for the editor. Give as full a reason as possible. The take might have been good until the end, when the noise of a car intruded. Write that down. The director might have been dissatisfied with an actor's performance or the cameraman with his framing. Write down the cause, whatever it is.

False starts

The director calls 'action' to start the shot but after a few seconds the actor might fluff his lines. Instead of 'cutting' the camera and starting again with a new take number the director might tell the actor to start again while the camera is still running. Make a note of that false start.

Duration

Give a timing for each take, from the moment the director says 'action' to when he says 'cut'.

PRODUCTION			EPISODE	SCENE	SLATE / IDENT
ROSES ARE RED				10	SHOT 42
NUMBER 34907		DATE 1·5·89			

FILM CAMERA ROLL	FILM SOUND ROLL	VIDEOTAPE REEL NUMBER 21907	(Circle whichever is appropriate) (INT.) DAY (NIGHT) / EXT (Weather)	(SYNC) GUIDETRACK WILDTRACK / MUTE PLAYBACK

LOCATION / SHOT DESCRIPTION

W/A living room (Roger's house)

CAMERA INFORMATION (If appropriate)
LENS
DISTANCE
STOP
FILTERS

TIMECODE OR ENDBOARD	TAKE*	DURATION	REMARKS (Reason if take is NG)	CONTINUITY NOTES (Including costume/props/dialogue/drawings etc.)
11:02:23	1	33"	performance	Costume notes see shot 40.
11:03:15	2	30"	light in shot	N.B fire lit, ditto candles.
11:04:10	3	35"	front OK. End NG dialogue	from: start scene
11:05:05	(4)	32"		to: "Why don't you then?"
	5			
	6			
	7			
	8			
	9			
	10			

* Circle acceptable takes - if more than 10 takes, use second sheet.

© Avril Rowlands 1989

135

Writing on the Script

As well as making notes on the continuity report form you should use your script in noting down continuity points. The great advantage of writing on the script lies in the fact that you can match the action to the dialogue with great accuracy.

Abbreviations of words and the use of symbols will enable you to write quickly on the script. Some people use a form of shorthand.

Below are a few commonly used abbreviations and symbols:

CR   Camera right
CL   Camera left
R   Right—from the actor's point of view
L   Left—from the actor's point of view
     (You might prefer to use the abbreviations R and L for camera right and left and r and l referring to right and left from the actor's point of view.)
X   Could be used to denote 'crosses', i.e. Fred X R—Fred crosses camera right, or to denote 'exits' or 'extra', i.e. XXR—extra exits camera right.
f/w Forwards
b/w Backwards
i/f   In front
b/h Behind
f/g   Foreground
b/g Background
An arrow can be used to denote a turn, a stand or a sit. ⤸ ↓

A stick man can be used to show arm movements. This is very useful when you want to note whether someone is eating, drinking or smoking.

Dialogue changes
It is part of your job to keep a note of dialogue changes, and you should keep your script up to date as these changes occur.

THE ADVERTISEMENT

LAURA IS SITTING BEHIND HER DESK, A DESK LITTERED
WITH PAPER AND PHOTOGRAPHS. EVEN THE CHAIR IS
FULL OF PAPERS. THERE IS A KNOCK ON THE DOOR.

Writing r. hand.
looks up.

LAURA *looks down. carries on writing*
Come in!

bag held on
r. arm.

P. x R

PAULINE ENTERS THE ROOM AND APPROACHES LAURA'S
DESK.

PAULINE
I've come about the advertisement. *bag to shoulder*

LAURA *(head down)*
Just a minute. (SHE FINISHES WHAT SHE IS WRITING,
THEN LOOKS UP) Sorry about that. You've come
about...?

PAULINE *advertised*
The advertisement. You know, the one in the
paper.

LAURA
Oh, of course!

SHE SHAKES HANDS
P bag to floor *L picks up pen*
Do sit down. Just put that junk anywhere. ~~always work in an awful mess, don't you?~~ Now,
you're...?

PAULINE
Pauline. Pauline Lunt.

Other Paperwork

Daily continuity log

A daily log should be kept of the shooting, in shooting order. This should consist of the roll numbers, the slate number or timecode, the scene and the takes. This could prove very useful if you need to refer to a specific shot and only know that it was Slate 63.

Daily progress report

In the feature-film industry the production office will require a daily progress report to be compiled by the person doing continuity. These are more or less complex documents (the example given opposite is a simple version), which can include a comprehensive breakdown of every minute of time spent on location.

The progress report provides the production office with information on the times of shooting, for possible overtime payments, together with details of time spent in meals, in setting up and in any technical holdups. It also shows how much edited material has been shot each day, comparing it with the overall running time of the film, the amount already shot and the amount left to do, as well as giving the number of scenes covered each day, any retakes and any wildtracks.

Examples of daily continuity log and daily progress report

Date: 3.4.89

Production Number: 6581

TITLE: THE GERONIMO AFFAIR

SLATE	TAKE	SCENE	CAMERA ROLL NO.	SOUND ROLL NO.
324	1	45	16	9
"	2	"	"	"
"	3	"	"	"
325	1	46	16	9
326	1	12	16	9
"	2	"	17	"
"	3	"	"	"
"	4	"	"	"
327	1	"	"	10
"	2	"	"	"
"	3	"	"	"
"	4	"	"	"
"	5	"	"	"
328	1	"	"	"
329	1	"	18	"
340	1	13	"	"
"	2	"	"	"
"	3	"	"	"
"	4	"	"	"
"	5	"	"	"
"	6	"	"	"
"	7	"	"	11
341	1	13	"	"
342	1	"	"	"
"	2	"	"	"

SHOOT CALL:	0800	**DATE:**	3.4.89
1st SHOT:	0915	**PRODUCTION NUMBER:**	6581
LUNCH:	1255		
1st SHOT:	1445		
DINNER:	1830		
1st SHOT:	2025		
CAMERA WRAP:	2200		
SOUND WRAP:	2145		

	PAGES	SCENES	MINUTES
TOTAL SCRIPT	64	40	30
SHOT PREVIOUS	20	15	10.15"
SHOT TODAY	5	1	3.15"
TOTAL TO DATE	25	16	13.30"
TO DO	39	24	16.30"

SCENES COVERED	RETAKES	WILDTRACKS
6	–	14X – 20X

Information For the Editor

There are two ways of providing the editor with all the information he requires when working on a scripted production.

Typed-up continuity report sheets

You can type up all your rough notes on to a continuity report sheet and give it to the editor. That is the system most people follow and one which I used myself for many years until I happened to mention to my husband, who is a film and videotape editor, that all the additional typing in hotel bedrooms late at night or early in the morning were, for me, the one big drawback to the job.

His reply surprised me, for he said that he did not need half the information which had been so painstakingly given to him. For example, he was not interested in knowing what costumes the artistes wore—provided that continuity of costume was correct from shot to shot and scene to scene. Likewise the full description of the shot did not interest him. He did not need to be told that Jim entered shot frame L—walked R to the table—sat down—picked up the full glass of beer (with his right hand) etc. He had only to look at the relevant piece of film or tape to find all that out!

So together we devised a far simpler way of providing the editor with the information he really does need.

Continuity cards

The cards contain only the barest information about the shot, but it is information which the editor really needs. He needs to know which scene the shot relates to—the slate number or 'in' point of timecode, the camera or tape roll number and the sound roll number. Make a note if the take is sync or mute and use a separate card for wildtracks. Apart from that, he wants a brief description of the shot, e.g. W/A Henry's kitchen, and then, and vitally important to the editor, he needs to know about the takes: how many there were, which were NG and why, and which were acceptable. He needs nothing else *except* an accurate marked-up coverage script to tell him what the shot covers in the scene.

The cards are simplicity itself. You will find that you have time during the day to write them out, reasonably clearly and legibly, and if you are working on a series or inserts for a series, I find that different coloured cards corresponding to the colours of the scripts are useful.

Having gone on at some length about the virtues of using cards, it is only fair to say that some editors do not like working with cards—they prefer pieces of paper which they can then place in a file. There is, of course, no reason why the basic information the editor needs should not be written on pieces of paper rather than cards. The important point is to give the editor the information he wants and not a lot of extraneous detail which he will never look at, but which has caused you hours of unnecessary work.

Continuity sheet for the editor

Title ....

....

Date ....

EPISODE	SCENE	SLATE

Camera roll*	Sound roll*	Circle whichever is appropriate:
		SYNC GUIDE PLAY MUTE WILDTRACK
		TRACK BACK (to cover)

SHOT DESCRIPTION

Take*	Duration/ footage	Remarks (give full reason if take is NG)
1	* circle accepted takes	
2		

Continuity card

Slate	Ep/Scene	Neg. roll	Tape roll

Description

Take	1	2	3	4	5
Duration					
Remarks					

Coverage Scripts

If you use the card system of continuity then it really is very important that you give the editor an accurate marked-up coverage script together with the cards so that he can see what the shot covers in the scene.

Even if you do not use the card system, but type up continuity report sheets for the editor, he will find coverage scripts useful and you and the director might also find it helpful to have a marked-up script for yourselves.

On a copy of the script you should draw lines for each shot showing the total coverage of the scene. Identify each line by using different colours and write the slate number or 'in' point of timecode alongside, together with a brief description.

Do *not* draw a line for each take, just for each shot. Draw the lines on the left-hand side of the script, keeping them clear of the dialogue and mark any dialogue changes in the copy for the editor.

If this coverage script is accurate it will be of immense value to the editor and will also show you and the director the coverage of any scene at a glance.

Don't confuse this coverage (sometimes called a 'tramline') script with a possible cutting order which the director might provide for the editor.

Example of coverage script

SCENE 7 : GORE'S KITCHEN
          INT. DAY

THE ROOM IS NOW A SHAMBLES.
MRS GORE PRESENTS NICKY WITH
SOME BREAD AND BUTTER AND SOME
MILK. MRS GORE IS VERY DISHEVELLED
AND DISTRAIT. SHE LOOKS AS IF SHE
HASN'T SLEPT.

MRS GORE

That's all there is. We can't

cook anything now and even the

milk won't keep long now.

SHE GIVES AN UNHAPPY LOOK AT THE
FRIDGE WHICH IS STANDING WITH ITS
DOOR OPEN AND ITS SHELVES OUT.

NICKY

I'm now hungry anyway.

SHE DRINKS THE MILK

NICKY

I'd better go now.

MRS GORE

What?

SHE SUDDENLY TAKES IN THAT NICKY
IS DRESSED FOR SCHOOL.

MRS GORE

Nicky, you can't go to school.

68 Tracking 2-s

69 CU Mrs Gore
70 CU Nicky

72 MS Nicky → 2-s

Shot Listing

If you are working on an unscripted production the shot list you compile during shooting will be of vital importance to the director, the editor and the person who writes the commentary. It should therefore contain as much information as possible and be typed out neatly after shooting. Any interviews should be transcribed and attached to the shot list.

When shot listing you should note the following:

Location

Slate number or 'in' point of timecode
Give these details together with the number of takes.

Shot description
Make this as concise as possible while describing the shot accurately. Always write down the different stages of a developing shot and note especially how the shot begins and ends.

Sound
When shooting on film always note whether the shot is taken sync or mute and note down any wildtracks.

Duration
Time the duration of the shot and note that down.

Interviews
At some stage or other you will almost certainly be shot listing for an interview. There are one or two things to note about it.

Unless you are extraordinarily good at shorthand, or the interviewee speaks very slowly, you are unlikely to get it all down on paper. You can either take a tape or cassette recorder and make a rough recording which you can transcribe later, or it might be sufficient just to take note of the questions and the beginnings and ends of the answers.

The questions are important, as very often the interviewee is shot first, then one or two 'noddies', as they are called, are shot. These are shots of the interviewee, not talking, but listening. Then the camera might be turned round and the shots taken of the interviewer asking questions, with a few 'noddies' at the end. It is important therefore that you know exactly what questions were asked. Finally, or at the beginning, a wide-angle establishing shot is taken.

"STATELY HOMES"   Dir: Peter McDonnell   21st February 1986

Programme number: 21Z/367942/B   VTR No: 31548

Location: Withyton House, Staffs

T/C 'IN'	TAKE	SHOT DESCRIPTION	DUR.	OK/NG
10.05.00	1	EXTERIOR: HOUSE & GROUNDS		
		Wide establishing shot of house from gates - looking down tree lined drive	.45	OK
10.12.05	1	Z/O from house to WS a/b	1.00	NG - person in shot
10.16.20	2	a/b	1.05	OK
10.32.45	1	Start wide and z/i to house	.20	NG - cam
10.43.40	2	a/b	.55	OK
		EXTERIOR : SUNKEN GARDEN		
11.55.10	1	WS panning L-R to gazebo	.40	NG - cam wobble
11.57.28	2	a/b	.42	OK
12.14.48	1	WS panning R-L (starting on gazebo)	.47	OK

INTERIOR : DRAWING ROOM

Interview with Lord and Lady Corley

14.35.20	1	2-s Lord and Lady Corley on sofa		

Q: Lord and Lady Corley, this beautiful house is an amalgamation of many different styles of architecture. When was the first building constructed?

A: (Lord C) There has been a house on this site since Elizabethan times...west wing.. fire...restoration in Jacobean times..bits added by each succeeding generation.

Q: And have you added anything?

A: (Lady C) The vegetable garden and sunken garden altered   6.40   OK

The Realities of it All

Location work can be very tough. You will undoubtedly feel many times that there are easier ways of earning a living as you stand half-frozen and soaked to the skin in a field at three in the morning trying to shoot a group of sheep who refuse to cross the field from left to right. Or when you are lost in a mist on the hills with a director who has lost the map, lost his and everybody else's way, and, even more important, lost the location caterers who are somewhere down in the valley.

Continuity itself is hard work. It requires an immense amount of concentration, not only when shooting is actually taking place, but when nothing is apparently happening and most of the unit appear to be idling around. Most of them *are* idling around, but if the director and cameramen are working, then you must be working too.

Continuity also involves sitting up typing and marking up editing scripts often into the small hours while everyone else relaxes, enjoyably fraternising with the local populace.

If, however, you feel I have drawn too black a picture, do not forget that if you *do* prove to be one of those strange people like myself who love the work, and find continuity a most satisfying job, you will find like-minded people on every new unit.

And the discomforts? . . . Well they do make for good after-dinner stories.

'. . . you see, there I was, standing quietly watching the action, when I felt something tugging my hand. And it was this goat we'd borrowed from the local farmer to use as dressing. You know what it was up to? It was quietly eating my continuity notes in a contented sort of way . . .'

1

2

3

4

The realities of shooting
1. Shooting can be frustrating
2. It can be annoying—when the director has lost the way
3. It can be hard work—typing at night when everyone else relaxes
4. But it does provide good after-dinner stories

Post Production

It is very easy, at the 'end-of-production party', to think that all the work is over. The artistes are leaving, their minds on their next role, or lack of one; the crews are busy thinking and talking about their next job. The sets are dismantled and the costumes and props returned to the hire companies. The close-knit unit, so like a family in its internal working, is splitting up and there is a general air of relief at a job completed and the thought of returning to civilisation, tinged with sadness at the ephemeral nature of the business.

You prepare the paperwork for the editor and, apart from tidying up loose ends, might also feel that the production is over. But for many people the end of shooting signifies the start of their job. Unless editing has been taking place at the same time as shooting, the work of the editor starts when your job ends.

Editing

What has been recorded on film or videotape is a mass of unrelated material, shot out of sequence. It is now the job of the editor, working creatively with the director, to reassemble this material into its final story order. The picture will be edited, the sound mixed together and captions or graphics added before the production can be called complete.

Principles of editing

The mechanics of editing, i.e. the equipment used and the application of that equipment, will differ greatly according to whether film or videotape is being edited, but the basic principles of editing remain the same.

Likewise, an editor might be working for months on end on a multi-million-pound feature film, involving innumerable tracks of stereo sound and specially scored music, or on a pop promotion involving complex digital effects or just be engaged in videotape editing at its most basic, whereby the editor mixes together the sound track consisting of location sound and a commentary at the same time as editing the picture, but the principles of editing are the same.

The editor's role is to juxtapose visual images and sound creatively and dramatically so that a story is told in sound and pictures.

'The editor working creatively with the director.'

Editing the Picture

Film

When you record on videotape the picture and sound are on the same tape or cassette and you can play them back straightaway. When using film the pictures are shot by the camera onto film stock and the sound is recorded on a separate tape recorder onto quarter-inch wide magnetic tape. The sound can be played back immediately but the picture cannot until the exposed film has been processed at a film laboratory.

Before any editing can take place the sound has to be re-recorded onto magnetic sound film, of either 16 mm or 35 mm width, usually according to the gauge used for the picture. Once this is done, the picture and sound are synchronised by the film editor's assistant then viewed by the producer, the director and the film editor so that the final selection of takes may be made. After viewing, the editor breaks down the rolls of picture and sound, physically cutting them up into individual shots for easy access and the editing process begins.

The editing is done by joining these shots together in whatever order is decided upon by the director and editor. Shots can be experimented with in any order, and they can be lengthened, shortened, replaced or re-cut at any point. When using negative/positive film stock it does not matter what state the print gets into: it is only a guide for the negative cutter who splices the negative *only* after all the creative decisions have been made. This system allows immense flexibility. It means that changes can be made at any time until the negative is cut. Once the negative is cut, the show print or prints can be made without loss of picture quality, since they are made directly from the picture negative.

Videotape

At first sight, videotape editing seems to be simpler. Sound and picture are already in sync on the same roll or cassette and all the editor has to do is to re-record the sections wanted in the right order onto another roll of tape. This would give us pictures and sound of second generation. The problem is that all the editing decisions have to be right first time, and all have to be made in story order, since to go back and make alterations without doing all the work again means going to a new generation of tape. Each time material is copied onto a new generation you lose both picture and sound quality. The way round this problem is by off-line editing.

Off-line editing

This means that the original material is copied onto some inferior format, usually VHS, and the timecode which has been recorded onto the master tape would be 'burned in' to this copy. The copy can then be edited, going to as many generations as necessary, as the quality of the picture is irrelevant. Sophisticated off-line systems, such as 'Elitrack', record on computer disc all the edit decisions throughout all the generations.

150

Once all the decisions have been made, the master tape will be edited at the 'on-line' editing session. There will then be only one generation between the original and the transmitted tape.

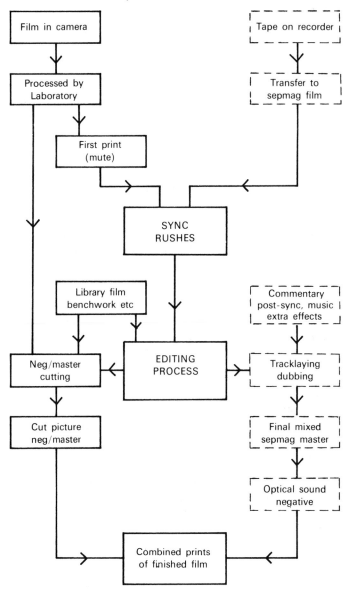

Film: editing picture and sound
This is what happens to the film after a day's shooting.
In television, the show print is usually mute and is shown in conjunction with the final sepmag track on a double-head machine.

Editing the Sound

Film
It is important to remember that you cannot record anything in a film-cutting room. All the sound required—actuality sound shot on location, sound effects, music, commentary, wildtracks, etc.—have to be transferred to magnetic sound film of the same gauge as the picture and laid onto tracks, in sync with the picture. A dubbing cue sheet is prepared by the editor and the dubbing mixer works from this when mixing the various tracks together to form one master sound track. This operation takes place in a dubbing theatre.

Videotape
Very often in videotape editing all the various sounds required in the finished production are mixed together by the editor at the same time as he edits the picture. Alternatively, tracks can be laid rather like on film, except that they are re-recorded in sync with the master tape by the editor and finally mixed together in a dubbing theatre in much the same way as film.

What does a PA do?
The PA might be required to find library effects, tapes or discs for the dubbing session. During the final run-through of the master sound track the PA should time any music for copyright purposes.

Pre-dubbing script
The script is merely an accurate shot list of the edited production, with the relevant film footage or edited tape timecode given on one side. In the case of timecode it is often more convenient for the hours and frames to be left off, i.e. 10 : 11 : 09 : 18 is written as 11 : 10. You should write the footage or timecode from the start of the first shot. This script can be used for writing commentary.

Commentary script
If the PA is required to type a script for the commentary it should be in treble spacing, with the footage or timecode on the left-hand side. A wide margin should be left for notes and alterations. Sentences should never be carried forward from one page to another.

Pre-dubbing post-production script

Shot No.	Description	Footage
1	W/A harbour	000
2	LS boat about to dock	032
3	MS man walking down gangplank	041
	(steps onto land) S/I MAIN TITLE	047
4	Man walking onto railway platform	064
5	LS train coming into station	092
6	Train stops, man gets in	119
7	L/A train departing	143
8	Int. train. Man speaking SYNC	168
9	B/W Library shot. LMS steam train	182

Commentary script

TIMECODE	COMMENTARY
11 : 10	NARRATOR: I'm now going to travel on the wildest
	railway line in Great Britain, part of which was
	originally called the Duke of Sutherland's railway.
	When the line was built, it had a private station
	at Dunrobin to serve the Duke's castle. That
	station's still there.

(clear by 11 : 26 for train effects)

(11 : 43   TO CAM. IN TRAIN
There's even a buffet car on this amazing service
which runs three times a day but never on Sundays.
Before the war they served kippers.)

Copyright: 1

Copyright is the protection the law (in the UK, the Copyright Act 1956) gives to a person or organisation for something that they have created.

Protection
The protection the law gives ensures that no one other than the copyright owners have the right to use the work unless authorised by the owner, who is thus able to charge a fee. It is particularly important that permission is obtained before any material is used in a production if that material is copyright.

Simple copyright
In its simplest form the material could be a literary work, a painting, a photograph, a musical composition or a recorded musical performance. But such things as records, illustrated books, films and videos involve multiple copyright.

Multiple copyright
Let us take the example of a film. Copyright in a film belongs to the film maker. However, it is not as simple as that, as the film distributor may have bought some or all the rights in that film. For example, the film *Heavens Above* was a Boulting Brothers production, distributed to cinemas by British Lion Films and available on 16 mm for non-theatrical use by Filmbank Distributors Ltd. Before using an excerpt of this film in another production one has to trace which organisation is in a position to give the necessary permission.

Suppose a brasswear manufacturer had bought the rights to include an excerpt of *Heavens Above* in a corporate video called *Brass* because they had made the altar candlesticks seen in the film. No one, including the brasswear manufacturer, has the right to use that sequence in any other video without negotiating fresh rights from British Lion, even though they may have copied the sequence from *Brass*. The brasswear manufacturer does not own the copyright of the sequence, only a licence permitting him to use it in *Brass*.

Copyright extends for 50 years from the film being registered under Part III of the Cinematographic Films Act 1950 (UK), or, if not registered, 50 years from when it was first published, i.e. when copies were sold or hired to the public.

Music copyright

A commercial recording involves multiple copyright: the composers'; the performers'; the recording company's.

Copyright: 2

Photographs
Copyright extends for 50 years from when the photograph was first published.

Artistic works
Copyright extends for 50 years from the year of the author's death.

Music
The composer's copyright extends for 50 years from the death of the composer. But be careful, because if the work has since been re-arranged by someone, the arranger enjoys the same copyright protection as the original composer.

With gramophone records the copyright resides with the gramophone manufacturers for 50 years from when the recording was first published.

Literary works
Copyright extends for 50 years from the end of the year in which the author died.

One final word. If, say, an artist is commissioned to do a work, then the copyright of that work may well rest with the person or organisation who commissioned it and not with the artist.

NOTE: All references to copyright made here apply to the law in force in the UK, although *in general* they apply in the US also.

Literary works
Copyright extends for 50 years after the death of the author.

Post Production Script

Throughout this book you have probably been aware that a large part of your job has been to record events. These may be events that have not yet taken place, as with the shooting schedule; those that are in the process of taking place, as with the continuity report sheet or the shot list; or events that have already taken place, as with the post production script.

This script is the written account of the production. It contains *everything* that is in the finished production and, more than that, it comprises the source of everything you have used, whether it be specially shot for the production, film archive material, music or photographs.

Use of the script

The post production script has a twofold use:

1. It is used for costing purposes. As it contains the original source of everything used in the production, including details of the artistes, it makes the job of paying the correct people relatively simple.
2. It is used for archive purposes. If anyone in future years wishes to use any part of the material it will be easy for them to find all the requisite details from this script.

What the script contains

The script contains all the action (in the form of a shot list), together with the dialogue, against the film footage or timecode reference.

Library film

If library film is used, this is shown and the copyright source given.

Music

Full details of all music must be given—whether it is specially composed or taken from a commercial recording, in which case details of the maker, the performers, the composer and the record publisher must be given.

Photographs

The original source of all photographs must be given.

Post production script

Footage	Action	Sound
000	W/A harbour	Natural F/X and music "The Three Elizabeths" Suite Comp. & cond. Eric Coates Orchestra: The New Symphony DECCA LK 4056
032	LS boat about to dock	
041	MS man walking down gangplank	
047	Isteps on to land) S/I MAIN TITLE	
064	Man walking on to railway platform	Music ends 064 - train F/X only
092	LS train coming into station	
119	Train stops, man gets in	COMM: I'm now going to travel on the wildest railway line in Great Britain, part of which was originally called the Duke of Sutherland's railway. When the line was built it had a private station at Dunrobin to serve the Duke's castle. That station's still there.
143	L/A train departing	F/X train departing
168	Int. Train. Man speaking	SYNC DIALOGUE: There's even a buffet car on this amazing service which runs three times a day but never on Sundays. Before the was they served kippers.
182	B/W Library shot. LMS Steam train near Altnabreac (Private collection: R. McTavish, 4 Shaw St. Lochinver, Sutherland)	Music "The Four Centuries Suite" Comp. & cond: Eric Coates Orchestra: The New Symphony DECCA LK 4056

159

Film and Videotape Formats

Film

If the production is being shot on film it will be either shot on 16 mm or 35 mm wide film stock: 35 mm film stock is of better quality and is used for feature films, TV commercials and pop promotions. Some very high budget TV productions are shot on 35 mm, but 16 mm is the standard for television.

Videotape

It was recently said in jest that as 35 mm film has been an industry standard for over 80 years, two-inch quadruplex videotape an industry standard for 20 years, and one-inch helical scan videotape a standard so far for 10 years, if the present profileration of videotape formats continues, by the turn of the century a broadcast VTR will have to be capable of changing format during playback, as the average life of a video format will be less than the running time of a tape!

In the last few years, as video equipment has become more portable, a wide range of recording formats has emerged, some very much more successful than others. To help readers find their way through the maze of shapes and sizes, below is a list of formats and their applications at the time of writing (November 1990).

Two-inch quadruplex

For many years this was the only broadcast standard. It is now virtually obsolete apart from archive purposes. Archive material in the UK recorded on early 405-line black and white machines are not in any way compatible with later 625-line two-inch machines.

One-inch Helical scan

This superseded two-inch videotape in the later 1970s. Although once regarded as the broadcast standard, it is being superseded by Betacam SP, M2 or one of the digital formats.

Two and one-inch videotapes come on spools. All other formats are cassette based.

Three-quarter-inch Low-Band U-matic

This is used professionally but is not of broadcast standard.

Three-quarter-inch High-Band U-matic

This is a development of Low-Band that gives a (just) broadcast-quality picture.

Three-quarter-inch SP High Band

A 'superior performance' version of High Band giving better picture quality.

Half-inch Betacam

The first truly portable broadcast-quality format which allows the use of a camcorder. Betacam pictures are very much better than U-matic but still do not meet full broadcast engineering specifications.

Half-inch Betacam SP

A spectacular improvement on Betacam giving full broadcast-quality pictures from a cassette format.

Half-inch M2

A rival to Betacam SP.

All the above recording systems are analogue, which means that each time the pictures are re-recorded they are degraded to a greater or lesser extent. Studio broadcast VTRs in the future will be digital recorders. This means no degradation on editing or copying. Three systems so far have been developed: D1 (for component signals), and D2 (for composite signals). Although both these two systems use three-quarter inch tape in cassettes, they are not compatible with each other nor, of course, with the U-matic formats. The third digital format is D3, sometimes known as DX, which uses half-inch tape in cassettes.

Domestic systems

Half-inch VHS and Super VHS
Half-inch Betamax
Video-8